AWAKEN DREAM JOURNAL

I0807064

PAIGE COLLINS

AWAKEN
DREAM JOURNAL

UNDERSTANDING
GOD'S VOICE
IN YOUR DREAMS

WHITAKER
HOUSE

Unless otherwise indicated, all Scripture quotations are taken from *The Passion Translation*®. Copyright © 2017, 2018, 2020 by Passion & Fire Ministries, Inc. Used by permission. All rights reserved. ThePassionTranslation.com. Scripture quotations marked (NLT) are taken from the *Holy Bible, New Living Translation*, copyright © 1996, 2004, 2015 by Tyndale House Foundation. Used by permission of Tyndale House Publishers, Inc., Carol Stream, Illinois 60188. All rights reserved. Scripture quotations marked (NIV) are taken from the *Holy Bible, New International Version*®, NIV®, © 1973, 1978, 1984, 2011 by Biblica, Inc.® Used by permission of Zondervan. All rights reserved worldwide. www.zondervan.com. The "NIV" and "New International Version" are trademarks registered in the United States Patent and Trademark Office by Biblica, Inc.® Scripture quotations marked (KJ21) are taken from *The 21St Century King James Version*, © 1994 by Deuel Enterprises, Inc. Used by permission. All rights reserved. Scripture quotations marked (AMP) are taken from *The Amplified® Bible*, © 2015 by The Lockman Foundation, La Habra, CA. Used by permission. (www.Lockman.org). All rights reserved. Scripture quotations marked HCSB are taken from *the Holman Christian Standard Bible*®, copyright © 1999, 2000, 2002, 2003, 2009 by Holman Bible Publishers. Used by permission. *Holman Christian Standard Bible*®, Holman CSB®, and HCSB® are federally registered trademarks of Holman Bible Publishers. Scripture quotations marked (NKJV) are taken from the *New King James Version*, © 1979, 1980, 1982 by Thomas Nelson, Inc. Used by permission. All rights reserved. Scripture quotations marked (ESV) are taken from *The Holy Bible, English Standard Version*, © 2000, 2001, 1995 by Crossway Bibles, a division of Good News Publishers. Used by permission. All rights reserved.

AWAKEN DREAM JOURNAL
Understanding God's Voice in Your Dreams

Paige Collins

ISBN: 979-8-88769-459-7
eBook ISBN: 979-8-88769-460-3
Printed in the United States of America
© 2025 by Paige Collins

Whitaker House
1030 Hunt Valley Circle
New Kensington, PA 15068
www.whitakerhouse.com

Library of Congress Control Number: 2025903823

No part of this book may be reproduced or transmitted in any form or by any means, electronic or mechanical—including photocopying, recording, or by any information storage and retrieval system—without permission in writing from the publisher. Please direct your inquiries to permissionseditor@whitakerhouse.com.

1 2 3 4 5 6 7 8 9 10 11 32 31 30 29 28 27 26 25

CONTENTS

INTRODUCTION
7

DREAM JOURNAL WITH PROMPTS
27

PRAYERS
149

APPENDIX A: DICTIONARY OF TERMS
155

APPENDIX B: NUMBERS IN DREAMS
201

APPENDIX C: FURTHER READING AND SCRIPTURES
213

APPENDIX D: WORLD-CHANGING CHRISTIANS WHO WERE IMPACTED BY DREAMS
219

ABOUT THE AUTHOR
224

INTRODUCTION

Research has shown that nearly everyone dreams while they sleep, and some studies indicate that up to 95 percent of people dream regularly. *But do our nighttime visions and images hold any meaning for our waking lives?*

As it turns out, millions of people are asking this same question.

Google Trends (which tracks trends in online searches) revealed that beginning in spring of 2016, there was a slow and steady global rise in inquiries for the phrase "dream spiritual meaning" and related topics. Then, in the summer of 2020, an abrupt increase in these searches occurred as the line graph jolted upward sharply and continued to rise. At the time of this writing, Google Trends indicates that inquiries about dreams have fluctuated between 75 and 100 percent since the search engine began tracking trends in 2004.

There is an "awakening" happening—and not just in the United States. Globally, people appear to be dreaming more than ever before. If we consider nothing more than basic search engine analytics, we find that people around the world are having dreams they believe to be significant—dreams that *mean something*. If you're reading this book, you likely are one of those people.

Given that dreams are shrouded in mystery and symbolism, it's no surprise that in response to the growing interest, New Age and Eastern gurus have flooded the marketplace with guides, websites, and journaling products written from a non-biblical and often occult-centered worldview. While some symbolism can seem universal, it's vitally important that we seek to understand our dreams through a Christ-centered, biblical lens. Alternative resources offering counterfeit "truths" can be dangerous, leading readers to skewed and tainted answers for very legitimate questions that only the Holy Spirit can answer.

The Bible is filled with examples of God using dreams to speak prophetically, issuing warnings, revealing hidden truths, and communicating about important things to come. Nearly every major character in the Bible heard from God in a dream or vision at one time or another. The Creator of the universe still speaks to those made in His image through dreams and visions. The apostle Peter reminded the early church at Pentecost the words of Joel, "*This is what I will do in the last days—I will pour out my Spirit on everybody and cause your sons and daughters to prophesy, and your young men will see visions, and your old men will experience dreams from God*" (Acts 2:17).

Visions and dreams are byproducts of His Spirit.

WHY DREAMS AND WHY NOW?

We've established, at least anecdotally, that God-inspired dreams are on the rise in our day. But why? I have a theory. In a fast-paced digital world, I believe these dreams are on the rise due to increased cultural "noise" levels.

TikTok, the short-form video social media app, rose to popularity in 2018, when it became the most downloaded app in the United States. It has continued to grow in popularity since then, becoming the most downloaded app in the world in 2020, 2021, and 2022, boasting nearly 1.6 billion active users. Recent data show that the average American spends *seven hours and three minutes* on screens per day (the global average is about the same), split between social media and streaming entertainment. Our eyes and ears are constantly intercepting chatter—our culture is loud. However, in 1 Kings 19, the prophet Elijah describes the voice of God as a "*gentle whisper*" (1 Kings 19:12 NLT).

How are we going to hear a whisper amid the booming chaos of modern-day media? Our minds and spirits are only ever truly quiet when we are sleeping. I believe God is invading our sleeping hours—when no other distractions are competing for our attention—to speak and encounter His people.

I know what you must be asking: "If God wants to speak to us, why would He communicate in such a cryptic way? Why speak through veils and shadows in the night?" The answer is simple: intimacy. Uncovering the meaning behind what seems to be a cryptic language requires us to draw very, *very* close. And closeness—relationship—is what God desires more than anything else.

> *God conceals the revelation of his word in the hiding place of his glory. But the honor of kings is revealed by how they thoroughly search out the deeper meaning of all that God says.*
> —Proverbs 25:2

It is an honor to seek out the deeper things of God. As we sit with Him, talking, asking questions, and, most important, drawing near to listen, we encounter a kind and loving Father and Friend who is eager to share secrets with us, His beloved children. It's from the seat of intimacy—of knowing and being fully known in His love—that we are healed, delivered, unburdened, and empowered to advance His kingdom in the earth.

I believe that He so passionately wants to have our attention that He will speak in our night seasons in order that we might become aware of His voice and seek to know Him more.

WHY DREAM JOURNALING?

This dream journal is a specialized tool. It's not just a place to record the things you see and experience while you're asleep. It's a tool forged to help you discern the voice of God in your life and explore one of the miraculous and beautiful ways He communicates with us. Over time, your dream journals will become the written record of a personal conversation you've had with the Creator of the universe!

Keeping a dream journal enables us to zero in on the patterns and symbols that appear (and sometimes repeat) in our dreams as we seek revelation from the Holy Spirit to uncover what He might be saying. It also allows us to keep track of all that God is saying so that, in the future, we can look back and remember all He has accomplished in and through us.

Some of the most remarkable and beautiful moments of my life began with a dream.

If you're new to the concept of God-dreams, even the idea that He speaks to people in this way might sound odd or even superstitious. However, as previously mentioned, the Bible is full of examples of God using dreams to speak to people about things to come, as well as to offer warnings. But, as we've established, spiritual dreams are not just some dusty language lost to the pages of Scripture—the Author of dreams still uses them to reveal wisdom for our daily lives, relationships, and, yes, even the future.

I will never forget my first "God-dream." It was the first of hundreds to follow—and it was different from any dream I had experienced before. I had always been a dreamer of sorts—you know, normal dream stuff…mosaics of seemingly random thoughts and experiences mushed into weird narratives. Nothing worth remembering (or so I thought). I certainly had never imagined that God would speak to me through a dream.

One night, that changed—I had a powerful dream. As I was waking up, I heard the sound of my own voice, praying out loud and asking God for an interpretation of the dream. When I fully came to, I knew God had done something new in me. I had woken up in a state of prayer, after all!

I immediately had the urge to record the dream, so I grabbed a basic lined journal and wrote down everything I could remember. That notebook became my first dream journal. From that point, the dreams kept coming, I continued to record them, and a sort of "training" began.

When that journal was completely full, I bought another. Before I knew it, I had a drawer filled with notebooks. With the Holy Spirit as my guide, along with a few biblically based resources, I learned the spiritual significance of my dreams and the objects and symbols within them, and soon developed my method of diagramming each dream.

Over the years, God has revealed various aspects of my vocational calling while I slept, with accuracy that would blow your mind. I have dreamed dozens of warnings about people and situations, for myself and others—many of these are too personal to share in a public forum. Numerous times, I have come face-to-face with the demonic in a dream—something that feels terrifying in the moment but builds faith and courage, even while I'm sleeping.

Through dreams, God has encouraged me countless times and even shown me promises over my life. I remember a season when the company I own was going through an unexpected financial crisis, and I found myself in constant prayer over it. One morning, as I was waking up in that lucid state—you know, when you're not fully asleep and yet not quite awake—I heard a voice: "Give Me forty-one days to turn it around."

I knew God was preparing me to witness a financial miracle that only He could do. Sure enough, forty-one days later, every revenue projection for our year had not only increased but had also doubled, almost to the penny, month over month.

God has also administered healing through dreams. For example, one night in a dream, a faceless woman (whom I believe represented an angel, per Psalm 91:11) came to me and simply said, "The flu is coming." After she spoke those words, she looked down at my hand, which I was now holding out in front of me; I opened it, and in my palm were five pills. Instinctively, I swallowed them, and immediately my eyes opened wide awake. I heard the sound of chattering teeth. My four-year-old son, who at the time was sleeping on a pallet on the floor by my bed (a toddler phase), was shivering, burning with fever.

Now, thanks to the dream I'd just had, I already knew what we were dealing with (the flu). But when I woke him to administer Tylenol, he promptly sneezed in my face. (I literally felt the spray land in my mouth...the life of a parent!) The next morning, I took him with me to the clinic; no surprise, we both tested positive for the flu. I was early in my symptoms and only experiencing mild achiness and fatigue; my son, on the other hand, had a very high fever that was not responding to medication. At one point, I even had to put him in a lukewarm bath to try to bring his temperature down. Every mother knows the heartache of seeing your little one miserably sick.

As I remembered my dream, I recalled being given what looked like medicine, which I had taken. *One important principle to always keep in mind with dreams, visions, or other types of revelations you receive from God is this: He reveals to heal.* Meaning, He is diagnostic *and* prescriptive—if you are shown a problem, then He intends to provide a solution.

This dream was not for my amusement. It served as an opportunity to put my faith into action and believe in God's healing for me and my son. I began to pray out loud in my home, saying, "Lord, thank You for dreams and revelation. Right now, I come into agreement with Your healing power. As a daughter of the King of Kings, and with the authority empowered unto me by Your Holy Spirit, I release the angels who are on assignment in my home to heal and minister to my family. I bind all sickness and curse the flu virus in the name of Jesus, and I decree and declare that no weapon formed against us will prosper, in Jesus's name."

Within an hour or so, my son's fever broke and did not return, and my symptoms never even developed! The next day, we left for our scheduled family vacation and had a great time.

Now, don't hear what I'm *not saying*, which is that every ailment will be healed supernaturally. We have had the flu before and taken Tamiflu to treat it. We have had COVID-19 and taken Paxlovid. We have seen illnesses and injuries that require medicine, rest, stitches, and casts. What I *am saying*, however, is that sometimes God will reveal to you the solution to a problem or the outcome of a future situation. In these instances, it's your responsibility to *agree in faith* in spite of whatever is happening in the natural and call forth what He has shown you. (See Romans 4:17.) My child had the flu—he was burning with fever—but I knew what God had shown me, and His reality is *more real* than what we can see with our natural eyes. As I came into agreement with what He had shown me in the dream, and declared it, the natural circumstances shifted. He gives us opportunities to partner with Him to see His power and to increase our faith—and we respond by giving Him the glory.

Let's look at a story from Scripture to further illustrate this point, because I think it's one of the most critical aspects of our dreaming life. In Acts 23, after Roman soldiers took the apostle Paul into custody, the Lord appeared to him one night, saying, "*Take courage! As you have testified about me in Jerusalem, so you must also testify in Rome*" (Acts 23:11 NIV). This promise from God assured Paul that he would indeed make it to Rome. When he finally set out on the journey (see Acts 27), the ship carrying Paul and the other prisoners encountered a terrible storm. Again, an angel appeared to Paul in the night and assured him that they all would survive. Although the boat shipwrecked, all of the passengers made it safely to land, where they began to build a fire to warm themselves. As Paul was putting wood on the fire, a deadly viper was driven out by the flames and bit him on the hand. What did Paul do? He just shook it off into the fire. God had already told him he would stand trial in Rome—he knew this journey would end with him standing in front of Caesar and testifying about Jesus, not dying on a beach from a snake bite. The promise of God was his protection.

Dreams can also reveal important future life events. In February 2021, I had a dream in which my husband was driving a truck down a windy two-lane road, and I was sitting in the passenger seat. Suddenly, he jerked the wheel, taking us off the road and into a field with endless rows of small corn sprouts. One of the details I noticed was the size of the corn—small sprouts only about six inches high, indicative of late-spring growth. We drove through the farmer's field, cutting deep ruts into the soil, and came to a locked gate that led to the road. In order for us to leave the field, the farmer would have to come and unlock the gate. In the dream, I felt restless, impatient, and ready to get out of there. Ultimately, the farmer did come to unlock the gate, and we were free to go. The dream ended.

A month later, my husband was recruited by a company in Omaha, Nebraska, famously home of the Cornhuskers. We moved in June of that year, and our neighborhood was surrounded on four sides by—you guessed it—corn fields. I couldn't help but notice the size of the corn when we arrived—about six inches high. Not long after we moved there, I felt restless and uncomfortable—the winters were too cold for this Southern girl, building and establishing a community of faith and friendships felt hard, and I was a long way from my family. After a few months, I was *so* ready to leave that place, but, as I reflected on the dream I'd had, I knew we would live in Omaha until God—represented by the owner of the field, the "farmer"—opened the gate (metaphorically) and released us in His timing. The dream had shown me our relocation to Omaha, revealed that I wouldn't necessarily be happy there, and also reassured me that there would eventually be an end to that season.

Another type of God-dream is a *warning*. I have probably had more warning dreams than any other kind! These dreams are intended to reveal a forthcoming threat and prepare you spiritually for it. Warning dreams may involve situations that make you feel afraid, chaotic, or on edge. Most of the time, these warnings represent events in the natural realm that will threaten to harm you in some way. You might dream about snakes, spiders, or wolves, or even tornadoes, floods, or terrorists. Hear me on this: 99 percent of the time, these events are symbolic. For example: If you dream about an earthquake, it's most likely symbolic of a forthcoming *shaking* in your life; if you dream of being bitten by a poisonous snake, you will probably feel the effects of sharp, hurtful, or "biting" words or lies (*where* you're bitten or stung on your body also holds symbolism as to how the event will affect you in the natural; hands can represent our "work" or the way we "serve," feet can represent our "walk," and so on).

Remember, the enemy is a predator—a devourer—and a thief whose only aim is to steal, kill, and destroy us and whatever we hold dear. (See John 10:10.) Sure, this includes our physical bodies, our loved ones, career, personal relationships, and possessions, but also our peace, joy, love, character, and integrity. But, again, we find that God *reveals to heal*. If He is kind enough to forewarn us of coming trouble, we can be assured our lives and situations are in His hands. Warning dreams remind us to put on the full armor of God, pray against evil, guard our hearts, and remain vigilant so that we do not walk into the traps of the enemy.

In a crisis, we can so quickly spiral into fear, say and do things out of anger, and *react* to threatening circumstances in ways that don't align with the kingdom of God, which, in turn, can create more problems. Just as people who live in coastal communities prepare in advance for a hurricane, when God warns us in advance of a coming threat, we can be ready to weather the storm by preparing spiritually.

Here is an example of a warning dream I once had:

> I'm with a group of people, a wedding party, and the sky grows dark. A very loud and violent tornado approaches, and we all run into buildings made of glass. I know they will not offer us any protection, but the tornado dissipates, and we are all okay.

This dream actually made me very nervous. I had this dream two weeks before I was supposed to travel to England for a friend's wedding. As I considered it, I prayed over my travel, my friendships, the bride and groom, and so forth, but never I felt a clear understanding of what this warning meant. A couple of days into the weeklong trip in the UK, the wedding party was hit with a short-lived but violent norovirus that took several of us out for twenty-four hours. There was really no avoiding it, and in the end, we all bounced back, and the wedding proceeded as planned.

Sometimes, you may fully understand a dream only *after* certain events have taken place that help connect all of the dream symbolism to reality. Hindsight revelation is a helpful tool in learning *your specific* dream language.

Dreams can also be used to expose unhealed wounds of the heart, lies we're believing, and even hidden sins that, for many reasons, we can't even see ourselves. Dreams like these are not meant to shame us. Again, *He reveals to heal*—therefore, our dreams will sometimes shine a light on uncomfortable areas of our lives in order for us to see them clearly, as He does, so that we can bring these issues to His feet. Like a deep splinter, we can learn to live with something uncomfortable—becoming so accustomed to its presence, we don't even know it's there. But He has come that we may have abundant life. (See John 10:10.) When we ask, He reveals deeper things inside us that are not aligned with His heart, and He may do this through a dream. When we have knowledge and understanding of the issue, we can be led through the necessary healing or repentance and into fuller life.

You may ask, "But how do I know my dream is from God, and not just random?"

First and foremost, I believe that most dreams have meaning and are worth unpacking, but random thoughts, feelings, and memories can clutter them. My question for you is: What are you taking in through your eyes and ears during the day? Have you ever noticed on social media that when you click on a cute puppy video, the platform then starts offering you more cute puppy videos? Your choices seep into your feed, and the algorithm shifts to accommodate your viewing habits.

Our dreams can be like that. If it's true that *you become what you behold*, then inevitably you will also dream about those things. Sorting through a junk-filled dream is like picking through a garage sale, looking for treasures, and it's a process that requires wisdom and discernment from the Holy Spirit.

One of the first things God showed me in a dream was that He wanted me to set aside all my other books and forms of entertainment, except for the Bible, for a season. For about six months, I turned off social media, stopped watching shows and other forms of entertainment, and spent time in Scripture. Now, He had me on this journey for a specific reason—there were things He wanted to show me in the story of His people that would inform the next season of my life. I had been given a clear directive for a specific purpose. But the larger effect this media fast had on my dream life during that season was extreme. My dreams were powerful, clear, vivid, and pure. This was the season when God revealed to me, in dreams, my greater purpose and calling. I didn't have to wonder if my subconscious was pulling from something I'd seen on TV or in a movie, because I was fasting from those things. Though my dreams did require interpretation, my intimacy with Him had been nurtured, and our dialogue around dreams seemed to flow with ease.

God can and will certainly break through the clutter, but if you are passionate about hearing Him through dreams, I would recommend pairing this journal with a media detox and a season of meditating on the Word of God.

> *So may the words of my mouth, my meditation-thoughts, and every movement of my heart be always pure and pleasing, acceptable before your eyes, Yahweh, my only Redeemer, my Protector.* —Psalm 19:14

DREAM SYMBOLISM 101: HOW GOD USES SYMBOLISM

God uses symbolism throughout Scripture to help communicate to His prophets. In Jeremiah 1, He becomes an instructor in the interpretation of His symbolic language when He *establishes* young Jeremiah as a prophet for Israel.

In the story, God first proclaims, "*I knew you before I formed you in your mother's womb. Before you were born I set you apart and appointed you as my prophet to the nations*" (Jeremiah 1:5 NLT). At first, Jeremiah protests that he's too young to speak for God, but the Lord doubles down, reconfirming His decision to send Jeremiah as His messenger to Israel *now* (rather than waiting until he was older, as was the custom). He anoints Jeremiah's mouth to speak with authority, then gives the young prophet a crash course on how to see and interpret visions.

> *The word of the Lord came to me, saying, "Jeremiah, what do you see?" And I said, "I see the branch (maqqēl) of an almond tree* [šāqēd]*." Then the Lord said to me, "You have seen well, for I am [actively] watching* [šōqēd] *over My word to fulfill it."* —Jeremiah 1:11–12 AMP

In the vision, God shows Jeremiah the branch of an almond tree, then explains to him that it represents His vigilance, or His "watching." The Hebrew word for almond tree (*shaqed*) *is pronounced almost identically to* the word for "watching" (*shoqed*). In this way, the Lord uses a play on words. He shows Jeremiah an object that, when spoken out loud, *sounds like something else*. Sometimes when we speak our dreams out loud, we find truths hidden in the words.

There is another layer of significance to the vision of the staff (*maqqēl*) of almond wood that would not have been lost on Jeremiah or the early Jewish readers of this sacred story, especially *in the context* of this particular conversation, where God is giving Jeremiah a new identity and authority. If we go back and read Numbers 17, we find another story where God uses a branch to establish authority in a leader He has chosen for His people. As recorded in Numbers 17, after much bickering among the people, the Lord causes Aaron's "staff" to bud like the branch of a tree as a sign to all of Israel that he was God's choice as the high priest. Jeremiah would have heard this story many times throughout his life and would have understood that with one symbolic image of the almond branch, the same God who confirmed Aaron's priesthood was also confirming him as a prophet.

God then gives Jeremiah a second vision with symbolism that is more overt and *easier* to understand. The symbolism still requires interpretation, but there are no puns or cryptic messages here:

> *Then the Lord spoke to me again and asked, "What do you see now?" And I replied, "I see a pot of boiling water, spilling from the north." "Yes," the Lord said, "for terror from the north will boil out on the people of this land. Listen! I am calling the armies of the kingdoms of the north to come to Jerusalem. I, the Lord, have spoken!"* —Jeremiah 1:13–15 NLT

Jeremiah's "training" shows us that some dreams will be obscure, while others will be straightforward. This story also presents a basic model for interpreting dreams or visions. Notice the structure of this lesson, because the same process applies to our own process. This simple process is meant to be a dialogue; let God teach you as He did Jeremiah.

First, God reveals something to us in a vision or dream.

Second, we *confirm, identify, speak out loud, write down, describe*, and so on, what we've seen.

Third, He explains, interprets, and clarifies the meaning for us.

I love so many things about this story—Jeremiah's very human insecurity and pushback, the Lord's patient and practical instruction—but, mostly, it's the personal, conversational dynamic between them that stirs me. I hope you will lean into this story and allow it to encourage you in your own journey as you engage the Lord for the interpretation of your dreams.

APPLY THE LAW OF FIRST MENTION

The Law of First Mention is a principle used in biblical interpretation that suggests that the first time a concept, word, number, or other element appears in the Bible, it often establishes the most basic and straightforward meaning. The idea holds that God intentionally sets a precedent for a concept the first time it's introduced in Scripture, and that can offer us a clear understanding of its intended purpose.

When you are researching the symbols, names, numbers, and concepts from your dreams, start by applying the Law of First Mention. While the Law of First Mention is *not an absolute rule,* it's one of the many tools we can use when seeking to understand God's intention behind a symbol.

PRACTICAL EXAMPLES

Here are a few examples of how to apply the Law of First Mention to your dream symbols. The dream dictionary included in the back of this journal contains several common *biblical* objects and symbols with their possible meanings, primarily based on the Law of First Mention, but I encourage you to do your own research.

WATER: *"The earth was without form and void, and darkness was over the face of the deep. And the Spirit of God was hovering over the face of the waters"* (Genesis 1:2 ESV). Before God spoke light into existence or formed the earth's structure, there was water. Water is described as part of the unformed *"deep"* over which the Spirit of God/*Ruach*/breath of God hovers, or moves, symbolizing the raw material from which the Creator brought life. As one of the foundational elements of the created world, and essential for sustaining life, the first mention of water establishes it as a symbol of *life and creation,* and a *representation of God's Spirit,* as the Spirit of God hovers over it.

Throughout the Bible, water continues to symbolize *life, cleansing, renewal, judgment,* and the *Holy Spirit.* Let's examine some of its other references:

- **Sustenance:**
  - Water is essential for physical life and was a provision in the wilderness. (See Exodus 17:6.) Spiritually, water represents the nourishment God provides for the soul: *"Come, all you who are thirsty, come to the waters"* (Isaiah 55:1 NIV). In John 4:14, Jesus offers *"living water"* to the Samaritan woman, symbolizing eternal life and spiritual renewal.
- **Cleansing and Purification (physical and spiritual):**
  - In Leviticus 14:8–9, ritual washings symbolized purification from sin. The Word of God is described as the means by which Jesus Christ cleansed the church: *"by the washing with water through the word"* (Ephesians 5:26 NIV).
- **Deliverance:**
  - The Israelites' crossing of the Red Sea (see Exodus 14) symbolizes God's deliverance of His people from bondage.
- **Renewal and New Birth:**
  - *"He saved us through the washing of rebirth and renewal by the Holy Spirit"* (Titus 3:5 NIV). Jesus speaks of being *"born of water and the Spirit"* (John 3:5) as a requirement for entering the kingdom of God.
- **The Holy Spirit:**
  - *"Whoever believes in me, as Scripture has said, rivers of living water will flow from within them"* (John 7:38–39 NIV). By this, Jesus meant the Spirit.

FLOOD: With related, but mostly different, symbolism to that of water, a flood represents an *event*. The very well-known first mention of a *flood* is in the story of Noah, where God said:

> *I am going to release a great flood that will destroy all life upon the earth, and every breathing thing under heaven will perish—everything on earth will die. But as for you, I will establish my covenant of friendship, and you will escape destruction by coming into the ark, you and your wife, your sons and their wives.*
> —Genesis 6:17–18

God declares His intention to bring a flood to remove wickedness from the earth while preserving Noah and his family.

And so, a dream of a flood could speak of a forthcoming event that, though it may feel chaotic, will mark the *removal of that which offends the Holy Spirit* and a making way for a fresh start under God's covenant. Remember that which brought destruction to many, lifted Noah and his family higher (in the ark), and honored their friendship with God. Similarly, in 1 Peter 3:20–21, the flood is compared to baptism, symbolizing salvation through water and a *cleansing* from sin.

WINE: *"And Noah began to be a farmer, and he planted a vineyard. Then he drank of the wine and was drunk, and became uncovered in his tent"* (Genesis 9:20–21 NKJV). The first mention of wine in the Bible follows the flood, when Noah plants a vineyard and enjoys its fruit. The rest of Genesis chapter 9 goes on to highlight Noah's resulting drunkenness and the consequences when his son Ham dishonors him by exposing his nakedness.

So, based on the Law of First Mention, we find that wine represents *both* the fruits of our labor (vineyard cultivation) and also impaired judgment/consequences—a blessing and a potential stumbling block. We continue to see this duality recur in Scripture, as wine becomes a symbol of *joy*, covenantal *blessing*, and, at times, *divine judgment*. Here are some of the possible meanings and references:

- **Celebration, Joy, Provision:**
  - *"Wine that makes glad the heart of man"* (Psalm 104:15 NKJV).
  - John 2:1–11: Jesus's first miracle at Cana involved turning water into wine, symbolizing divine provision and the joy of the new covenant.
- **Covenant and Redemption:**
  - *"This cup is the new covenant in my blood, which is poured out for you"* (Luke 22:20 NIV).
- **Judgment and Wrath:**
  - The *"great winepress of the wrath of God"* (Revelation 14:19).
- **Warnings:**
  - *"Wine is a mocker, strong drink is a brawler, and whoever is led astray by it is not wise"* (Proverbs 20:1 NKJV).

CAR/VEHICLE: Though the Bible obviously doesn't mention such modern conveyances such as cars, the symbolism associated with these vehicles can be connected to their biblical equivalents, such as chariots, carts, or even animals used for travel. This approach helps link modern symbols to timeless truths of Scripture.

The first mention of a mode of transportation is in Genesis 45:19, where Pharaoh says to Joseph, *"Do this: Take some carts from Egypt for your children and your wives, and get your father and come"* (NIV). In this Scripture, we see Pharaoh provide carts for Joseph's family to move to Egypt during the famine.

In this first mention, the carts represent *provision*, the *facilitation of a journey*, and a *tool for accomplishing God's will* in preserving the family of Israel. We can draw a parallel between the first mention of this mode of transportation in Scripture and our modern modes of transportation. We can also examine the function and purpose of the vehicles in our dreams (i.e., a simple car, a used car, a fancy sports car, an SUV, a bus, and so on) to derive further meaning. Context is key.

PRACTICAL SYMBOLISM IN LIGHT OF THESE BIBLICAL PRINCIPLES:

- Vehicles/cars may symbolize journey, purpose, and the means of carrying out God's plan (the vehicle of your destiny).
- A new car might symbolize blessings, provision, or new beginnings.
- A broken-down or beat-up car could symbolize spiritual neglect or the need for restoration in your life. (Also, who is driving...? You? Someone else?)
- A sports car might represent a high-powered, fast-moving season of your spiritual life.
- A bus might represent being in community with others.
- A school bus might represent a teaching ministry or a season where you are learning alongside others.
- A journey in a vehicle can remind believers of their spiritual journey toward their eternal destination.

As with these, and hundreds of other examples, the context in which these symbols appear in your dream is important. Identifying all of the possible meanings of your dream symbols is like dumping out five hundred puzzle pieces on the table. Still, you will need the Holy Spirit to help you put it all together into one cohesive picture. Your part is to write it down, dissect it, and bring it to Him with awe, curiosity, and a heart to receive. His part is to be the Teacher and bring you full revelation.

HOW TO USE THIS DREAM JOURNAL

I have found that when I steward my dream life well, not only do I have more dreams, but I grow in intimacy with God. After years of filling lined notebooks with my dreams, I longed for a tool custom-created for this sacred practice that I could share with others. You're now holding that very tool in your hands, and I have more than a hunch that this process might change your life, too.

WRITE IT ALL DOWN

We tend to forget the content of our dreams shortly after waking. Good stewardship of your dreams involves writing them down right when you wake up—when they are still clear in your mind, and you're still *feeling* them. Don't discount cat naps or dreaming that can happen in that lucid state. I have had many profound encounters with the Lord during a quick twenty-minute snooze.

When it comes to writing down your dreams, it's important to remember this rule: *If you notice it, it matters.* Every detail you remember can have a purpose in the overall meaning of a dream. So, no matter how small it may seem, write down every detail that comes to mind. Sometimes it helps me to speak the dream out loud—there's something about hearing the sound of the words coming out of my mouth that registers awareness, especially with a play on words. (Example: "Biltmore" could be a play on words for "build more.")

Then, once you've recorded it all, review what you've written and underline anything symbolic—objects, places, names or people, locations, numbers that stand out, colors or color patterns, as well as your point of view in relation to everyone and everything else in the dream. (Example: Are you a third-person observer or an active participant?)

Start by identifying the recurring objects, names, and symbols in your dream that have personal significance for you. Ask yourself how those images make you *feel.* God knows you better than anyone, and He will use familiar images in familiar ways to speak to you. He speaks to each of us uniquely, through our dream "language"—our dreams are specifically tailored to our individual experience, contexts, and understanding. This means that the meanings associated with some symbols and themes that appear in my dreams may differ from those in your dreams.

For example, I love cats, and cats frequently appear in my dreams. As a child, I had a little cat whom I loved very much. I would dress her up in baby doll clothes and push her around in a stroller; she slept on my bed every night, bringing me a sense of comfort. When I see a cat, whether in the natural world or in a dream, I feel a sense of friendship. But suppose you're someone who dislikes cats or even has a fear of them; a cat in your dream would most likely represent something negative. Personal context is key.

When it comes to people, the same concept holds true. It's essential to evaluate how you feel about a person who appears in your dream and consider what they represent to you. Someone in a role of authority—a pastor, teacher, doctor, or parent—may represent God in any of His roles: Father, Teacher, Physician, Counselor, or Husband. Often, God will place certain people in a dream to communicate an idea or theme based on the meaning of a name. For example, my friend Kristi, who happens to be a Bible scholar, often appears in my dreams as a representation of Jesus Christ.

For this reason, I've included more than two hundred common names and their meanings in Appendix A: Dictionary of Terms in the back of this journal. Refer to this whenever it is helpful, but do not let it stand as the ultimate authority.

I've also included space to note colors or color schemes. Was your dream vibrant and bright? Did you glimpse the bluest sky or the greenest grass you've ever seen? Perhaps the scenes were cast in dystopian, sepia-toned shadows, possibly even in black-and-white. Maybe one item stands out as being *very* yellow, and, for some reason, that detail stays with you. Whatever the color patterns are, write them down, and refer to Appendix A in the back of the journal for any scriptural significance of specific colors. If the color is such that *you notice it*, it matters.

Another important consideration is any mention of specific numbers. You don't have to be a formally trained Bible scholar to understand that the Lord uses numbers symbolically throughout the Scriptures. There are some very concrete and objective meanings behind numbers that frequently show up in dreams. I've included some of these in Appendix B: Numbers in Dreams in the back of this journal.

Once you develop this practice, capturing these details will become second nature. One day, you'll realize that you speak the language of your dreams without even thinking about it.

What about nightmares? On occasion, I awaken with a start from something intense or scary. If this happens to you, immediately ask the Holy Spirit to give you a Scripture to anchor what you've just seen. There's something about those few seconds after waking up, when our conscious thoughts haven't had a chance to catch up with what our spirit has just experienced, when God's still small voice is *so* clear. You can never go wrong asking the Lord to speak through His Scriptures, and it goes without saying that if He whispers to you a Scripture verse, you should write it down.

You'll notice that I've included some useful prayers for dreamers throughout this book that you can use. One of these is "A Prayer Against Nightmares and Terrors." Feel free to borrow these as a starting point. Eventually, you will want to compose your own.

If you ever feel stuck, cross-reference the imagery in your dreams with other Bible-based resources that offer insight into name meanings, origins, or symbolism. Also, take an inventory of what each word might mean to you. I've also listed some additional resources in the back of this journal for exploring the spiritual significance of dreams. I limit my research to trusted, Scripture-backed sources, and use Google searches only for origin stories for names and locations.

Once you have curated the individual possible meanings and symbolism from your dream elements, stand back and consider them as a whole. What rises to the surface? What themes do you notice? Similar to looking down on a city from an airplane window, adjust your vision to see with a broader lens what might not be as obvious when you're immersed in the details.

Most importantly, take time to pray about your dream, asking the Holy Spirit to help you see any other clues you might have missed, and to understand not only the proper interpretation but also any relevant *applications*. How should the message be applied in your waking life? Ask the Teacher to teach you how to look at your dream.

PROCESS IN COMMUNITY

Do you have dreamer friends? Having one or two trusted friends with whom you can share your dreams can be a fun and helpful way to verbally process your dream and find clarity from it. I encourage you to learn alongside a few others, talk through some of the guided prompts in this book as a group, and support one another on your journey. The Holy Spirit speaks to those who have hearts to receive, and we each carry gifts meant to lift up and edify the body of Christ. Find some faithful dreamer friends and grow together as you learn to discern the voice of God in your dreams.

A PRACTICAL EXAMPLE

Here's a snippet from my dream journal, and my interpretation process that followed, which may provide some clarity about how this process works:

I am moving into Jonathan's apartment in New Hampshire; after I drop off my stuff, I travel into New York City to interview for a new job as a writer. The woman doing the hiring tells me she doesn't want to hire me as an employee; instead, she wants to partner together on a project.

As soon as I awoke, I grabbed my dream journal from my bedside table and wrote down every detail. Then, I began to review the details in pursuit of an interpretation. I first considered all of the symbolism and any repeating themes:

- Moving in with my friend Jonathan
- New Hampshire—New York—new job
- Writer—partnership—new project—publishing

I know that, typically, "moving/relocating" in a dream symbolizes transition, shifting, or even a new beginning. The fact that I'm joining my friend in his space suggests we will be in agreement on something. Though cities and locations *can* represent their literal real-life counterparts, I felt that, in this dream, New York and New Hampshire were symbolic: first, because Jonathan doesn't live in New Hampshire; second, because both cities have the word "New." The origin of the name New Hampshire means "new village." And from previous dreams, I've come to understand that, for me, New York usually represents commerce and business.

Once I had notated all of the relevant symbols and had broken them down individually, I stepped back as far as I could (metaphorically speaking) to "look" at the whole picture; the interpretation began to come into view. My mind and spirit swirled and chewed on the words "move," "new," "new project," "writer," and "publishing." A blurry image of "new" opportunities in publishing began to form. I stored this dream in my journal and my heart.

Weeks later, I began compiling my ideas for the *Awaken Dream Journal*. Initially, I intended to self-publish the book for my personal use, because *I needed it*. But then, one day, I found myself in an unrelated conversation with Jonathan (my friend and colleague from the dream above), and I casually mentioned my dream journal project. He happens to be a literary agent, and he made a startling suggestion, "I think you should partner with a publisher to share this dream journal with the world. And I will help you." I hung up the phone and ran to retrieve my dream journal, rereading the entry from so many weeks prior. Had I simply dismissed my dream as the result of random and meaningless thoughts, memories, and neurons converging during the night, I might have missed an opportunity to recognize the sweet conversation the Lord had started that night while I slept—one that whispered of something new.

You are holding this book because of a dream God gave me—a dream that I wrote down, considered, prayed through, and acted upon.

I love the way God speaks and don't want to miss one thing. I bet you don't, either. Your dreams will give you a deeper understanding of your spiritual gifts and callings. They will provide you with a greater sense of clarity, purpose, and alignment with God's will. Sometimes, they will be mere nudges toward something or someone God wants you to think about, pray for, or serve. At other times, they will be outright warnings that can save you from unnecessary pain and suffering. Some are prescriptive, others merely descriptive, but all are meant to engage you in a greater dialogue with God.

On a recent springtime biblical studies trip to Israel, our group explored many of the physical locations of Jesus's ministry. We visited sites in Galilee, Capernaum, Jerusalem, Caesarea Philippi, the Decapolis, and dozens of other historic locations in Israel and Palestine. We considered *where* He taught and *what* those hearing His voice would have been seeing with their eyes while listening to His words.

Often, Jesus used the varied visual landscape, including animals, plants, water, rocks, mountains, and familiar cultural ideas, to illustrate His teachings. His parables were filled with analogy, metaphor, and symbolism, borrowing from situations in the listeners' everyday lives—things they could see and understand in a personal way.

Our guide on this trip, my friend Kristi McLelland, explained, "If the students couldn't see it, the Teacher couldn't teach it."

A good example of this is Jesus's teaching on the kingdom of God being like a mustard seed. Spring in Israel is absolutely gorgeous, green, and lush. Fields of bright yellow mustard, which grows both cultivated and wild, can be seen across the landscape. More of a bush than a tree, mustard is a beautiful flowering plant that can spring up out of rocks as easily as it does on fertile ground, overtaking entire hillsides. Locals who would have heard Jesus's comparison would have understood that, like mustard, when the revelation of God's love is received, His kingdom spreads rapidly—like a weed.

As we reflect on our dreams, we should consider that the Holy Spirit is still using the same teaching techniques Jesus incorporated when He spoke to crowds or His disciples.

Our dreams will incorporate familiar people, ideas, and settings—these visuals are meant to help illustrate the point. Don't disregard the presence of any everyday associations—people, pets, places, and so on—simply because they're familiar and you see them on a daily basis. If you see them in your dreams, there's a reason.

My friend Candice often dreams about a family dog she once had, whose name was Justice. Like most family pets, he was a faithful friend. She's learned that when Justice appears in her dreams, he's a symbol of friendship, loyalty, and his namesake—justice. If you see something or someone familiar in a dream, consider their value and possible symbolism.

As Westerners, we often look for Bible stories to be true; however, in Middle Eastern culture, the story itself *is* the point. A Middle Eastern lens—the one through which Jesus taught and the Scriptures were written—would ask us to see and consider what is the *truth in the story*. Jesus's parables required listeners to go deeper in order to see what was under the surface.

In dream interpretation, this is our task and, quite frankly, our honor—to dig, to seek out and find the truth in the visions God gives us. To mine for what is hidden. *And then to respond,* whether it be with intercession for a friend, obedience in a big decision, or simply heeding a warning.

Though the *Awaken Dream Journal* is not an instruction manual for dream interpretation, I hope and pray it will become a treasured tool as you receive revelation through your dreams. I pray you will delve into the deep, seeking out the great secrets and mysteries of God and growing closer to Him in the process. I hope you fill boxes and shelves, year after year, with these treasured conversations, like I have. I don't know what awaits you as you sleep, but I know you're about to begin an exciting, divine adventure.

What will you do with the dreams God gives you?

You're about to find out.

DREAM JOURNAL WITH PROMPTS

DESCRIBE THE MOST VIVID PART OF YOUR DREAM. WHAT ARE SOME WAYS THIS SCENE COULD CONNECT TO YOUR CURRENT LIFE SITUATION?

WERE THERE ANY SPECIFIC SYMBOLS OR OBJECTS THAT STOOD OUT TO YOU? WHAT DO THEY MEAN TO YOU PERSONALLY? RESEARCH AND WRITE DOWN ANY BIBLICAL CONTEXT.

Jan | Feb | Mar | Apr | May | Jun | Jul | Aug | Sep | Oct | Nov | Dec

1 2 3 4 5 6 7 8 9 10 11 12 13 14 15 16 17 18 19 20 21 22 23 24 25 26 27 28 29 30 31

WRITE OUT THE ENTIRE DREAM BELOW

HOW DID YOU FEEL DURING THE DREAM, AND AFTER YOU WOKE UP?

DESCRIBE YOUR POV IN THE DREAM? (EX. ARE YOU WATCHING FROM THE OUTSIDE? OR AN ACTIVE PARTICIPANT?)

LIST ANY THEMES FROM YOUR DREAM THAT YOU MAY HAVE SEEN POP UP BEFORE - IN LIFE, OR IN A PREVIOUS DREAM. WHAT MIGHT THESE THEMES REPRESENT?

Title Your Dream: ______________________________

LIST ANY COLORS, NUMBERS, OBJECTS, NAMES OR PEOPLE FROM THE DREAM, FOLLOWED BY ANY POSSIBLE SYMBOLISM.

DESCRIBE THE SETTING OR LOCATION FOR THE DREAM. THIS CAN INCLUDE TONE OR COLORING.
(EX. THE SETTING WAS HAPPY AND COLORFUL, DREARY AND BLACK AND WHITE, OR CAST IN SEPIA TONES.) WHAT MIGHT THE SETTING SYMBOLIZE?

ASK GOD TO GIVE YOU A SCRIPTURE TO ANCHOR THE DREAM, AND WRITE BELOW.
(NUMBERS, ESPECIALLY, CAN OFTEN BE CONNECTED TO A SCRIPTURE REFERENCE.)

RECORD ANY OTHER NOTES, PRAYER POINTS OR REVELATION ABOUT YOUR DREAM BELOW.

WRITE YOUR INTERPRETATION BELOW.

Jan | Feb | Mar | Apr | May | Jun | Jul | Aug | Sep | Oct | Nov | Dec

1 2 3 4 5 6 7 8 9 10 11 12 13 14 15 16 17 18 19 20 21 22 23 24 25 26 27 28 29 30 31

WRITE OUT THE ENTIRE DREAM BELOW

HOW DID YOU FEEL DURING THE DREAM, AND AFTER YOU WOKE UP?

DESCRIBE YOUR POV IN THE DREAM? (EX. ARE YOU WATCHING FROM THE OUTSIDE? OR AN ACTIVE PARTICIPANT?)

LIST ANY THEMES FROM YOUR DREAM THAT YOU MAY HAVE SEEN POP UP BEFORE - IN LIFE, OR IN A PREVIOUS DREAM. WHAT MIGHT THESE THEMES REPRESENT?

Title Your Dream: ______

LIST ANY COLORS, NUMBERS, OBJECTS, NAMES OR PEOPLE FROM THE DREAM, FOLLOWED BY ANY POSSIBLE SYMBOLISM.

DESCRIBE THE SETTING OR LOCATION FOR THE DREAM. THIS CAN INCLUDE TONE OR COLORING.
(EX. THE SETTING WAS HAPPY AND COLORFUL, DREARY AND BLACK AND WHITE, OR CAST IN SEPIA TONES.) WHAT MIGHT THE SETTING SYMBOLIZE?

ASK GOD TO GIVE YOU A SCRIPTURE TO ANCHOR THE DREAM, AND WRITE BELOW.
(NUMBERS, ESPECIALLY, CAN OFTEN BE CONNECTED TO A SCRIPTURE REFERENCE.)

RECORD ANY OTHER NOTES, PRAYER POINTS OR REVELATION ABOUT YOUR DREAM BELOW.

WRITE YOUR INTERPRETATION BELOW.

Jan | Feb | Mar | Apr | May | Jun | Jul | Aug | Sep | Oct | Nov | Dec

1 2 3 4 5 6 7 8 9 10 11 12 13 14 15 16 17 18 19 20 21 22 23 24 25 26 27 28 29 30 31

WRITE OUT THE ENTIRE DREAM BELOW

HOW DID YOU FEEL DURING THE DREAM, AND AFTER YOU WOKE UP?

DESCRIBE YOUR POV IN THE DREAM? (EX. ARE YOU WATCHING FROM THE OUTSIDE? OR AN ACTIVE PARTICIPANT?)

LIST ANY THEMES FROM YOUR DREAM THAT YOU MAY HAVE SEEN POP UP BEFORE - IN LIFE, OR IN A PREVIOUS DREAM. WHAT MIGHT THESE THEMES REPRESENT?

Title Your Dream: ___

LIST ANY COLORS, NUMBERS, OBJECTS, NAMES OR PEOPLE FROM THE DREAM, FOLLOWED BY ANY POSSIBLE SYMBOLISM.

DESCRIBE THE SETTING OR LOCATION FOR THE DREAM. THIS CAN INCLUDE TONE OR COLORING.
(EX. THE SETTING WAS HAPPY AND COLORFUL, DREARY AND BLACK AND WHITE, OR CAST IN SEPIA TONES.) WHAT MIGHT THE SETTING SYMBOLIZE?

ASK GOD TO GIVE YOU A SCRIPTURE TO ANCHOR THE DREAM, AND WRITE BELOW.
(NUMBERS, ESPECIALLY, CAN OFTEN BE CONNECTED TO A SCRIPTURE REFERENCE.)

RECORD ANY OTHER NOTES, PRAYER POINTS OR REVELATION ABOUT YOUR DREAM BELOW.

WRITE YOUR INTERPRETATION BELOW.

Jan | Feb | Mar | Apr | May | Jun | Jul | Aug | Sep | Oct | Nov | Dec

1 2 3 4 5 6 7 8 9 10 11 12 13 14 15 16 17 18 19 20 21 22 23 24 25 26 27 28 29 30 31

WRITE OUT THE ENTIRE DREAM BELOW

HOW DID YOU FEEL DURING THE DREAM, AND AFTER YOU WOKE UP?

DESCRIBE YOUR POV IN THE DREAM? (EX. ARE YOU WATCHING FROM THE OUTSIDE? OR AN ACTIVE PARTICIPANT?)

LIST ANY THEMES FROM YOUR DREAM THAT YOU MAY HAVE SEEN POP UP BEFORE - IN LIFE, OR IN A PREVIOUS DREAM. WHAT MIGHT THESE THEMES REPRESENT?

Title Your Dream: ____________________

LIST ANY COLORS, NUMBERS, OBJECTS, NAMES OR PEOPLE FROM THE DREAM, FOLLOWED BY ANY POSSIBLE SYMBOLISM.

DESCRIBE THE SETTING OR LOCATION FOR THE DREAM. THIS CAN INCLUDE TONE OR COLORING.
(EX. THE SETTING WAS HAPPY AND COLORFUL, DREARY AND BLACK AND WHITE, OR CAST IN SEPIA TONES.) WHAT MIGHT THE SETTING SYMBOLIZE?

ASK GOD TO GIVE YOU A SCRIPTURE TO ANCHOR THE DREAM, AND WRITE BELOW.
(NUMBERS, ESPECIALLY, CAN OFTEN BE CONNECTED TO A SCRIPTURE REFERENCE.)

RECORD ANY OTHER NOTES, PRAYER POINTS OR REVELATION ABOUT YOUR DREAM BELOW.

WRITE YOUR INTERPRETATION BELOW.

Jan | Feb | Mar | Apr | May | Jun | Jul | Aug | Sep | Oct | Nov | Dec

1 2 3 4 5 6 7 8 9 10 11 12 13 14 15 16 17 18 19 20 21 22 23 24 25 26 27 28 29 30 31

WRITE OUT THE ENTIRE DREAM BELOW

HOW DID YOU FEEL DURING THE DREAM, AND AFTER YOU WOKE UP?

DESCRIBE YOUR POV IN THE DREAM? (EX. ARE YOU WATCHING FROM THE OUTSIDE? OR AN ACTIVE PARTICIPANT?)

LIST ANY THEMES FROM YOUR DREAM THAT YOU MAY HAVE SEEN POP UP BEFORE - IN LIFE, OR IN A PREVIOUS DREAM. WHAT MIGHT THESE THEMES REPRESENT?

Title Your Dream: ______________________________

LIST ANY COLORS, NUMBERS, OBJECTS, NAMES OR PEOPLE FROM THE DREAM, FOLLOWED BY ANY POSSIBLE SYMBOLISM.

DESCRIBE THE SETTING OR LOCATION FOR THE DREAM. THIS CAN INCLUDE TONE OR COLORING.
(EX. THE SETTING WAS HAPPY AND COLORFUL, DREARY AND BLACK AND WHITE, OR CAST IN SEPIA TONES.) WHAT MIGHT THE SETTING SYMBOLIZE?

ASK GOD TO GIVE YOU A SCRIPTURE TO ANCHOR THE DREAM, AND WRITE BELOW.
(NUMBERS, ESPECIALLY, CAN OFTEN BE CONNECTED TO A SCRIPTURE REFERENCE.)

RECORD ANY OTHER NOTES, PRAYER POINTS OR REVELATION ABOUT YOUR DREAM BELOW.

WRITE YOUR INTERPRETATION BELOW.

WRITE DOWN ANY FEELINGS OR EMOTIONS YOU EXPERIENCED IN YOUR DREAM. DID YOU WAKE FEELING AT PEACE OR AGITATED? HOW DO THESE EMOTIONS RELATE TO YOUR WAKING LIFE?

DID YOU HEAR ANY WORDS OR PHRASES IN YOUR DREAM? WRITE THEM DOWN. CONSIDER ANY INSTANCES OF A PLAY ON WORDS THAT MIGHT BE APPLICABLE. REFLECT UPON THE SIGNIFICANCE OF THESE WORDS IN YOUR PERSONAL LIFE.

Jan | Feb | Mar | Apr | May | Jun | Jul | Aug | Sep | Oct | Nov | Dec

1 2 3 4 5 6 7 8 9 10 11 12 13 14 15 16 17 18 19 20 21 22 23 24 25 26 27 28 29 30 31

WRITE OUT THE ENTIRE DREAM BELOW

HOW DID YOU FEEL DURING THE DREAM, AND AFTER YOU WOKE UP?

DESCRIBE YOUR POV IN THE DREAM? (EX. ARE YOU WATCHING FROM THE OUTSIDE? OR AN ACTIVE PARTICIPANT?)

LIST ANY THEMES FROM YOUR DREAM THAT YOU MAY HAVE SEEN POP UP BEFORE - IN LIFE, OR IN A PREVIOUS DREAM. WHAT MIGHT THESE THEMES REPRESENT?

Title Your Dream: ______

LIST ANY COLORS, NUMBERS, OBJECTS, NAMES OR PEOPLE FROM THE DREAM, FOLLOWED BY ANY POSSIBLE SYMBOLISM.

DESCRIBE THE SETTING OR LOCATION FOR THE DREAM. THIS CAN INCLUDE TONE OR COLORING.
(EX. THE SETTING WAS HAPPY AND COLORFUL, DREARY AND BLACK AND WHITE, OR CAST IN SEPIA TONES.) WHAT MIGHT THE SETTING SYMBOLIZE?

ASK GOD TO GIVE YOU A SCRIPTURE TO ANCHOR THE DREAM, AND WRITE BELOW.
(NUMBERS, ESPECIALLY, CAN OFTEN BE CONNECTED TO A SCRIPTURE REFERENCE.)

RECORD ANY OTHER NOTES, PRAYER POINTS OR REVELATION ABOUT YOUR DREAM BELOW.

WRITE YOUR INTERPRETATION BELOW.

Jan | Feb | Mar | Apr | May | Jun | Jul | Aug | Sep | Oct | Nov | Dec

1 2 3 4 5 6 7 8 9 10 11 12 13 14 15 16 17 18 19 20 21 22 23 24 25 26 27 28 29 30 31

WRITE OUT THE ENTIRE DREAM BELOW

HOW DID YOU FEEL DURING THE DREAM, AND AFTER YOU WOKE UP?

DESCRIBE YOUR POV IN THE DREAM? (EX. ARE YOU WATCHING FROM THE OUTSIDE? OR AN ACTIVE PARTICIPANT?)

LIST ANY THEMES FROM YOUR DREAM THAT YOU MAY HAVE SEEN POP UP BEFORE - IN LIFE, OR IN A PREVIOUS DREAM. WHAT MIGHT THESE THEMES REPRESENT?

Title Your Dream: ___________________________

LIST ANY COLORS, NUMBERS, OBJECTS, NAMES OR PEOPLE FROM THE DREAM, FOLLOWED BY ANY POSSIBLE SYMBOLISM.

DESCRIBE THE SETTING OR LOCATION FOR THE DREAM. THIS CAN INCLUDE TONE OR COLORING.
(EX. THE SETTING WAS HAPPY AND COLORFUL, DREARY AND BLACK AND WHITE, OR CAST IN SEPIA TONES.) WHAT MIGHT THE SETTING SYMBOLIZE?

ASK GOD TO GIVE YOU A SCRIPTURE TO ANCHOR THE DREAM, AND WRITE BELOW.
(NUMBERS, ESPECIALLY, CAN OFTEN BE CONNECTED TO A SCRIPTURE REFERENCE.)

RECORD ANY OTHER NOTES, PRAYER POINTS OR REVELATION ABOUT YOUR DREAM BELOW.

WRITE YOUR INTERPRETATION BELOW.

Jan | Feb | Mar | Apr | May | Jun | Jul | Aug | Sep | Oct | Nov | Dec

1 2 3 4 5 6 7 8 9 10 11 12 13 14 15 16 17 18 19 20 21 22 23 24 25 26 27 28 29 30 31

WRITE OUT THE ENTIRE DREAM BELOW

HOW DID YOU FEEL DURING THE DREAM, AND AFTER YOU WOKE UP?

DESCRIBE YOUR POV IN THE DREAM? (EX. ARE YOU WATCHING FROM THE OUTSIDE? OR AN ACTIVE PARTICIPANT?)

LIST ANY THEMES FROM YOUR DREAM THAT YOU MAY HAVE SEEN POP UP BEFORE - IN LIFE, OR IN A PREVIOUS DREAM. WHAT MIGHT THESE THEMES REPRESENT?

Title Your Dream: ______________________________

LIST ANY COLORS, NUMBERS, OBJECTS, NAMES OR PEOPLE FROM THE DREAM, FOLLOWED BY ANY POSSIBLE SYMBOLISM.

DESCRIBE THE SETTING OR LOCATION FOR THE DREAM. THIS CAN INCLUDE TONE OR COLORING.
(EX. THE SETTING WAS HAPPY AND COLORFUL, DREARY AND BLACK AND WHITE, OR CAST IN SEPIA TONES.) WHAT MIGHT THE SETTING SYMBOLIZE?

ASK GOD TO GIVE YOU A SCRIPTURE TO ANCHOR THE DREAM, AND WRITE BELOW.
(NUMBERS, ESPECIALLY, CAN OFTEN BE CONNECTED TO A SCRIPTURE REFERENCE.)

RECORD ANY OTHER NOTES, PRAYER POINTS OR REVELATION ABOUT YOUR DREAM BELOW.

WRITE YOUR INTERPRETATION BELOW.

Jan | Feb | Mar | Apr | May | Jun | Jul | Aug | Sep | Oct | Nov | Dec

1 2 3 4 5 6 7 8 9 10 11 12 13 14 15 16 17 18 19 20 21 22 23 24 25 26 27 28 29 30 31

WRITE OUT THE ENTIRE DREAM BELOW

HOW DID YOU FEEL DURING THE DREAM, AND AFTER YOU WOKE UP?

DESCRIBE YOUR POV IN THE DREAM? (EX. ARE YOU WATCHING FROM THE OUTSIDE? OR AN ACTIVE PARTICIPANT?)

LIST ANY THEMES FROM YOUR DREAM THAT YOU MAY HAVE SEEN POP UP BEFORE - IN LIFE, OR IN A PREVIOUS DREAM. WHAT MIGHT THESE THEMES REPRESENT?

Title Your Dream: ____________________

LIST ANY COLORS, NUMBERS, OBJECTS, NAMES OR PEOPLE FROM THE DREAM, FOLLOWED BY ANY POSSIBLE SYMBOLISM.

DESCRIBE THE SETTING OR LOCATION FOR THE DREAM. THIS CAN INCLUDE TONE OR COLORING.
(EX. THE SETTING WAS HAPPY AND COLORFUL, DREARY AND BLACK AND WHITE, OR CAST IN SEPIA TONES.) WHAT MIGHT THE SETTING SYMBOLIZE?

ASK GOD TO GIVE YOU A SCRIPTURE TO ANCHOR THE DREAM, AND WRITE BELOW.
(NUMBERS, ESPECIALLY, CAN OFTEN BE CONNECTED TO A SCRIPTURE REFERENCE.)

RECORD ANY OTHER NOTES, PRAYER POINTS OR REVELATION ABOUT YOUR DREAM BELOW.

WRITE YOUR INTERPRETATION BELOW.

Jan | Feb | Mar | Apr | May | Jun | Jul | Aug | Sep | Oct | Nov | Dec

1 2 3 4 5 6 7 8 9 10 11 12 13 14 15 16 17 18 19 20 21 22 23 24 25 26 27 28 29 30 31

WRITE OUT THE ENTIRE DREAM BELOW

HOW DID YOU FEEL DURING THE DREAM, AND AFTER YOU WOKE UP?

DESCRIBE YOUR POV IN THE DREAM? (EX. ARE YOU WATCHING FROM THE OUTSIDE? OR AN ACTIVE PARTICIPANT?)

LIST ANY THEMES FROM YOUR DREAM THAT YOU MAY HAVE SEEN POP UP BEFORE - IN LIFE, OR IN A PREVIOUS DREAM. WHAT MIGHT THESE THEMES REPRESENT?

Title Your Dream: ______________________

LIST ANY COLORS, NUMBERS, OBJECTS, NAMES OR PEOPLE FROM THE DREAM, FOLLOWED BY ANY POSSIBLE SYMBOLISM.

DESCRIBE THE SETTING OR LOCATION FOR THE DREAM. THIS CAN INCLUDE TONE OR COLORING.
(EX. THE SETTING WAS HAPPY AND COLORFUL, DREARY AND BLACK AND WHITE, OR CAST IN SEPIA TONES.) WHAT MIGHT THE SETTING SYMBOLIZE?

ASK GOD TO GIVE YOU A SCRIPTURE TO ANCHOR THE DREAM, AND WRITE BELOW.
(NUMBERS, ESPECIALLY, CAN OFTEN BE CONNECTED TO A SCRIPTURE REFERENCE.)

RECORD ANY OTHER NOTES, PRAYER POINTS OR REVELATION ABOUT YOUR DREAM BELOW.

WRITE YOUR INTERPRETATION BELOW.

IDENTIFY ANY PEOPLE OR FIGURES IN YOUR DREAM. WHAT ROLE DO THEY PLAY IN YOUR LIFE? WHAT FEELINGS DO THEY STIR UP IN YOU? ASK GOD TO REVEAL THEIR SIGNIFICANCE—AND WHAT HE MIGHT BE TELLING YOU THROUGH THEM.

WAS THERE A PARTICULAR COLOR OR COLOR PALETTE THAT WAS PROMINENT IN YOUR DREAM? WRITE DOWN ANY COLORS OR HUES, BRIGHT OR MUTED. EXPLORE ANY BIBLICAL SIGNIFICANCE AND RELEVANCE TO YOUR LIFE.

Jan | Feb | Mar | Apr | May | Jun | Jul | Aug | Sep | Oct | Nov | Dec

1 2 3 4 5 6 7 8 9 10 11 12 13 14 15 16 17 18 19 20 21 22 23 24 25 26 27 28 29 30 31

WRITE OUT THE ENTIRE DREAM BELOW

HOW DID YOU FEEL DURING THE DREAM, AND AFTER YOU WOKE UP?

DESCRIBE YOUR POV IN THE DREAM? (EX. ARE YOU WATCHING FROM THE OUTSIDE? OR AN ACTIVE PARTICIPANT?)

LIST ANY THEMES FROM YOUR DREAM THAT YOU MAY HAVE SEEN POP UP BEFORE - IN LIFE, OR IN A PREVIOUS DREAM. WHAT MIGHT THESE THEMES REPRESENT?

Title Your Dream: ____________________

LIST ANY COLORS, NUMBERS, OBJECTS, NAMES OR PEOPLE FROM THE DREAM, FOLLOWED BY ANY POSSIBLE SYMBOLISM.

DESCRIBE THE SETTING OR LOCATION FOR THE DREAM. THIS CAN INCLUDE TONE OR COLORING.
(EX. THE SETTING WAS HAPPY AND COLORFUL, DREARY AND BLACK AND WHITE, OR CAST IN SEPIA TONES.) WHAT MIGHT THE SETTING SYMBOLIZE?

ASK GOD TO GIVE YOU A SCRIPTURE TO ANCHOR THE DREAM, AND WRITE BELOW.
(NUMBERS, ESPECIALLY, CAN OFTEN BE CONNECTED TO A SCRIPTURE REFERENCE.)

RECORD ANY OTHER NOTES, PRAYER POINTS OR REVELATION ABOUT YOUR DREAM BELOW.

WRITE YOUR INTERPRETATION BELOW.

Jan | Feb | Mar | Apr | May | Jun | Jul | Aug | Sep | Oct | Nov | Dec

1 2 3 4 5 6 7 8 9 10 11 12 13 14 15 16 17 18 19 20 21 22 23 24 25 26 27 28 29 30 31

WRITE OUT THE ENTIRE DREAM BELOW

HOW DID YOU FEEL DURING THE DREAM, AND AFTER YOU WOKE UP?

DESCRIBE YOUR POV IN THE DREAM? (EX. ARE YOU WATCHING FROM THE OUTSIDE? OR AN ACTIVE PARTICIPANT?)

LIST ANY THEMES FROM YOUR DREAM THAT YOU MAY HAVE SEEN POP UP BEFORE - IN LIFE, OR IN A PREVIOUS DREAM. WHAT MIGHT THESE THEMES REPRESENT?

Title Your Dream: ______________________________

LIST ANY COLORS, NUMBERS, OBJECTS, NAMES OR PEOPLE FROM THE DREAM, FOLLOWED BY ANY POSSIBLE SYMBOLISM.

DESCRIBE THE SETTING OR LOCATION FOR THE DREAM. THIS CAN INCLUDE TONE OR COLORING.
(EX. THE SETTING WAS HAPPY AND COLORFUL, DREARY AND BLACK AND WHITE, OR CAST IN SEPIA TONES.) WHAT MIGHT THE SETTING SYMBOLIZE?

ASK GOD TO GIVE YOU A SCRIPTURE TO ANCHOR THE DREAM, AND WRITE BELOW.
(NUMBERS, ESPECIALLY, CAN OFTEN BE CONNECTED TO A SCRIPTURE REFERENCE.)

RECORD ANY OTHER NOTES, PRAYER POINTS OR REVELATION ABOUT YOUR DREAM BELOW.

WRITE YOUR INTERPRETATION BELOW.

Jan | Feb | Mar | Apr | May | Jun | Jul | Aug | Sep | Oct | Nov | Dec

1 2 3 4 5 6 7 8 9 10 11 12 13 14 15 16 17 18 19 20 21 22 23 24 25 26 27 28 29 30 31

WRITE OUT THE ENTIRE DREAM BELOW

HOW DID YOU FEEL DURING THE DREAM, AND AFTER YOU WOKE UP?

DESCRIBE YOUR POV IN THE DREAM? (EX. ARE YOU WATCHING FROM THE OUTSIDE? OR AN ACTIVE PARTICIPANT?)

LIST ANY THEMES FROM YOUR DREAM THAT YOU MAY HAVE SEEN POP UP BEFORE - IN LIFE, OR IN A PREVIOUS DREAM. WHAT MIGHT THESE THEMES REPRESENT?

Title Your Dream: ____________________

LIST ANY COLORS, NUMBERS, OBJECTS, NAMES OR PEOPLE FROM THE DREAM, FOLLOWED BY ANY POSSIBLE SYMBOLISM.

DESCRIBE THE SETTING OR LOCATION FOR THE DREAM. THIS CAN INCLUDE TONE OR COLORING.
(EX. THE SETTING WAS HAPPY AND COLORFUL, DREARY AND BLACK AND WHITE, OR CAST IN SEPIA TONES.) WHAT MIGHT THE SETTING SYMBOLIZE?

ASK GOD TO GIVE YOU A SCRIPTURE TO ANCHOR THE DREAM, AND WRITE BELOW.
(NUMBERS, ESPECIALLY, CAN OFTEN BE CONNECTED TO A SCRIPTURE REFERENCE.)

RECORD ANY OTHER NOTES, PRAYER POINTS OR REVELATION ABOUT YOUR DREAM BELOW.

WRITE YOUR INTERPRETATION BELOW.

Jan | Feb | Mar | Apr | May | Jun | Jul | Aug | Sep | Oct | Nov | Dec

1 2 3 4 5 6 7 8 9 10 11 12 13 14 15 16 17 18 19 20 21 22 23 24 25 26 27 28 29 30 31

WRITE OUT THE ENTIRE DREAM BELOW

HOW DID YOU FEEL DURING THE DREAM, AND AFTER YOU WOKE UP?

DESCRIBE YOUR POV IN THE DREAM? (EX. ARE YOU WATCHING FROM THE OUTSIDE? OR AN ACTIVE PARTICIPANT?)

LIST ANY THEMES FROM YOUR DREAM THAT YOU MAY HAVE SEEN POP UP BEFORE - IN LIFE, OR IN A PREVIOUS DREAM. WHAT MIGHT THESE THEMES REPRESENT?

Title Your Dream: ______________________________

LIST ANY COLORS, NUMBERS, OBJECTS, NAMES OR PEOPLE FROM THE DREAM, FOLLOWED BY ANY POSSIBLE SYMBOLISM.

DESCRIBE THE SETTING OR LOCATION FOR THE DREAM. THIS CAN INCLUDE TONE OR COLORING.
(EX. THE SETTING WAS HAPPY AND COLORFUL, DREARY AND BLACK AND WHITE, OR CAST IN SEPIA TONES.) WHAT MIGHT THE SETTING SYMBOLIZE?

ASK GOD TO GIVE YOU A SCRIPTURE TO ANCHOR THE DREAM, AND WRITE BELOW.
(NUMBERS, ESPECIALLY, CAN OFTEN BE CONNECTED TO A SCRIPTURE REFERENCE.)

RECORD ANY OTHER NOTES, PRAYER POINTS OR REVELATION ABOUT YOUR DREAM BELOW.

WRITE YOUR INTERPRETATION BELOW.

Jan | Feb | Mar | Apr | May | Jun | Jul | Aug | Sep | Oct | Nov | Dec

1 2 3 4 5 6 7 8 9 10 11 12 13 14 15 16 17 18 19 20 21 22 23 24 25 26 27 28 29 30 31

WRITE OUT THE ENTIRE DREAM BELOW

HOW DID YOU FEEL DURING THE DREAM, AND AFTER YOU WOKE UP?

DESCRIBE YOUR POV IN THE DREAM? (EX. ARE YOU WATCHING FROM THE OUTSIDE? OR AN ACTIVE PARTICIPANT?)

LIST ANY THEMES FROM YOUR DREAM THAT YOU MAY HAVE SEEN POP UP BEFORE - IN LIFE, OR IN A PREVIOUS DREAM. WHAT MIGHT THESE THEMES REPRESENT?

Title Your Dream: ______________________

LIST ANY COLORS, NUMBERS, OBJECTS, NAMES OR PEOPLE FROM THE DREAM, FOLLOWED BY ANY POSSIBLE SYMBOLISM.

DESCRIBE THE SETTING OR LOCATION FOR THE DREAM. THIS CAN INCLUDE TONE OR COLORING.
(EX. THE SETTING WAS HAPPY AND COLORFUL, DREARY AND BLACK AND WHITE, OR CAST IN SEPIA TONES.) WHAT MIGHT THE SETTING SYMBOLIZE?

ASK GOD TO GIVE YOU A SCRIPTURE TO ANCHOR THE DREAM, AND WRITE BELOW.
(NUMBERS, ESPECIALLY, CAN OFTEN BE CONNECTED TO A SCRIPTURE REFERENCE.)

RECORD ANY OTHER NOTES, PRAYER POINTS OR REVELATION ABOUT YOUR DREAM BELOW.

WRITE YOUR INTERPRETATION BELOW.

REFLECT ON ANY ACTIONS YOU TOOK OR DECISIONS YOU MADE IN THE DREAM. HOW MIGHT THEY RELATE TO CHOICES YOU NEED TO MAKE IN YOUR WAKING LIFE?

DID YOU ENCOUNTER ANY CHALLENGES, OBSTACLES, OR THREATS IN YOUR DREAM? MOST OPPOSITION WILL SYMBOLICALLY REPRESENT THE "ENEMY," REGARDLESS OF ITS APPEARANCE. PRAY FOR DISCERNMENT TO UNDERSTAND HOW ANY CHALLENGES MAY MIRROR ANY CURRENT REAL-LIFE SITUATIONS AND HOW TO POSTURE YOUR HEART TO EXPERIENCE ANY FUTURE CONFLICTS.

Jan | Feb | Mar | Apr | May | Jun | Jul | Aug | Sep | Oct | Nov | Dec

1 2 3 4 5 6 7 8 9 10 11 12 13 14 15 16 17 18 19 20 21 22 23 24 25 26 27 28 29 30 31

WRITE OUT THE ENTIRE DREAM BELOW

HOW DID YOU FEEL DURING THE DREAM, AND AFTER YOU WOKE UP?

DESCRIBE YOUR POV IN THE DREAM? (EX. ARE YOU WATCHING FROM THE OUTSIDE? OR AN ACTIVE PARTICIPANT?)

LIST ANY THEMES FROM YOUR DREAM THAT YOU MAY HAVE SEEN POP UP BEFORE - IN LIFE, OR IN A PREVIOUS DREAM. WHAT MIGHT THESE THEMES REPRESENT?

Title Your Dream: ______________________________

LIST ANY COLORS, NUMBERS, OBJECTS, NAMES OR PEOPLE FROM THE DREAM, FOLLOWED BY ANY POSSIBLE SYMBOLISM.

DESCRIBE THE SETTING OR LOCATION FOR THE DREAM. THIS CAN INCLUDE TONE OR COLORING.
(EX. THE SETTING WAS HAPPY AND COLORFUL, DREARY AND BLACK AND WHITE, OR CAST IN SEPIA TONES.) WHAT MIGHT THE SETTING SYMBOLIZE?

ASK GOD TO GIVE YOU A SCRIPTURE TO ANCHOR THE DREAM, AND WRITE BELOW.
(NUMBERS, ESPECIALLY, CAN OFTEN BE CONNECTED TO A SCRIPTURE REFERENCE.)

RECORD ANY OTHER NOTES, PRAYER POINTS OR REVELATION ABOUT YOUR DREAM BELOW.

WRITE YOUR INTERPRETATION BELOW.

Jan | Feb | Mar | Apr | May | Jun | Jul | Aug | Sep | Oct | Nov | Dec

1 2 3 4 5 6 7 8 9 10 11 12 13 14 15 16 17 18 19 20 21 22 23 24 25 26 27 28 29 30 31

WRITE OUT THE ENTIRE DREAM BELOW

HOW DID YOU FEEL DURING THE DREAM, AND AFTER YOU WOKE UP?

DESCRIBE YOUR POV IN THE DREAM? (EX. ARE YOU WATCHING FROM THE OUTSIDE? OR AN ACTIVE PARTICIPANT?)

LIST ANY THEMES FROM YOUR DREAM THAT YOU MAY HAVE SEEN POP UP BEFORE - IN LIFE, OR IN A PREVIOUS DREAM. WHAT MIGHT THESE THEMES REPRESENT?

Title Your Dream: ______________________________

LIST ANY COLORS, NUMBERS, OBJECTS, NAMES OR PEOPLE FROM THE DREAM, FOLLOWED BY ANY POSSIBLE SYMBOLISM.

DESCRIBE THE SETTING OR LOCATION FOR THE DREAM. THIS CAN INCLUDE TONE OR COLORING.
(EX. THE SETTING WAS HAPPY AND COLORFUL, DREARY AND BLACK AND WHITE, OR CAST IN SEPIA TONES.) WHAT MIGHT THE SETTING SYMBOLIZE?

ASK GOD TO GIVE YOU A SCRIPTURE TO ANCHOR THE DREAM, AND WRITE BELOW.
(NUMBERS, ESPECIALLY, CAN OFTEN BE CONNECTED TO A SCRIPTURE REFERENCE.)

RECORD ANY OTHER NOTES, PRAYER POINTS OR REVELATION ABOUT YOUR DREAM BELOW.

WRITE YOUR INTERPRETATION BELOW.

Jan | Feb | Mar | Apr | May | Jun | Jul | Aug | Sep | Oct | Nov | Dec

1 2 3 4 5 6 7 8 9 10 11 12 13 14 15 16 17 18 19 20 21 22 23 24 25 26 27 28 29 30 31

WRITE OUT THE ENTIRE DREAM BELOW

HOW DID YOU FEEL DURING THE DREAM, AND AFTER YOU WOKE UP?

DESCRIBE YOUR POV IN THE DREAM? (EX. ARE YOU WATCHING FROM THE OUTSIDE? OR AN ACTIVE PARTICIPANT?)

LIST ANY THEMES FROM YOUR DREAM THAT YOU MAY HAVE SEEN POP UP BEFORE - IN LIFE, OR IN A PREVIOUS DREAM. WHAT MIGHT THESE THEMES REPRESENT?

Title Your Dream: ______________________________

LIST ANY COLORS, NUMBERS, OBJECTS, NAMES OR PEOPLE FROM THE DREAM, FOLLOWED BY ANY POSSIBLE SYMBOLISM.

DESCRIBE THE SETTING OR LOCATION FOR THE DREAM. THIS CAN INCLUDE TONE OR COLORING.
(EX. THE SETTING WAS HAPPY AND COLORFUL, DREARY AND BLACK AND WHITE, OR CAST IN SEPIA TONES.) WHAT MIGHT THE SETTING SYMBOLIZE?

ASK GOD TO GIVE YOU A SCRIPTURE TO ANCHOR THE DREAM, AND WRITE BELOW.
(NUMBERS, ESPECIALLY, CAN OFTEN BE CONNECTED TO A SCRIPTURE REFERENCE.)

RECORD ANY OTHER NOTES, PRAYER POINTS OR REVELATION ABOUT YOUR DREAM BELOW.

WRITE YOUR INTERPRETATION BELOW.

Jan | Feb | Mar | Apr | May | Jun | Jul | Aug | Sep | Oct | Nov | Dec

1 2 3 4 5 6 7 8 9 10 11 12 13 14 15 16 17 18 19 20 21 22 23 24 25 26 27 28 29 30 31

WRITE OUT THE ENTIRE DREAM BELOW

HOW DID YOU FEEL DURING THE DREAM, AND AFTER YOU WOKE UP?

DESCRIBE YOUR POV IN THE DREAM? (EX. ARE YOU WATCHING FROM THE OUTSIDE? OR AN ACTIVE PARTICIPANT?)

LIST ANY THEMES FROM YOUR DREAM THAT YOU MAY HAVE SEEN POP UP BEFORE - IN LIFE, OR IN A PREVIOUS DREAM. WHAT MIGHT THESE THEMES REPRESENT?

Title Your Dream: ______________________________

LIST ANY COLORS, NUMBERS, OBJECTS, NAMES OR PEOPLE FROM THE DREAM, FOLLOWED BY ANY POSSIBLE SYMBOLISM.

DESCRIBE THE SETTING OR LOCATION FOR THE DREAM. THIS CAN INCLUDE TONE OR COLORING.
(EX. THE SETTING WAS HAPPY AND COLORFUL, DREARY AND BLACK AND WHITE, OR CAST IN SEPIA TONES.) WHAT MIGHT THE SETTING SYMBOLIZE?

ASK GOD TO GIVE YOU A SCRIPTURE TO ANCHOR THE DREAM, AND WRITE BELOW.
(NUMBERS, ESPECIALLY, CAN OFTEN BE CONNECTED TO A SCRIPTURE REFERENCE.)

RECORD ANY OTHER NOTES, PRAYER POINTS OR REVELATION ABOUT YOUR DREAM BELOW.

WRITE YOUR INTERPRETATION BELOW.

Jan | Feb | Mar | Apr | May | Jun | Jul | Aug | Sep | Oct | Nov | Dec

1 2 3 4 5 6 7 8 9 10 11 12 13 14 15 16 17 18 19 20 21 22 23 24 25 26 27 28 29 30 31

WRITE OUT THE ENTIRE DREAM BELOW

HOW DID YOU FEEL DURING THE DREAM, AND AFTER YOU WOKE UP?

DESCRIBE YOUR POV IN THE DREAM? (EX. ARE YOU WATCHING FROM THE OUTSIDE? OR AN ACTIVE PARTICIPANT?)

LIST ANY THEMES FROM YOUR DREAM THAT YOU MAY HAVE SEEN POP UP BEFORE - IN LIFE, OR IN A PREVIOUS DREAM. WHAT MIGHT THESE THEMES REPRESENT?

Title Your Dream: ______________________________

LIST ANY COLORS, NUMBERS, OBJECTS, NAMES OR PEOPLE FROM THE DREAM, FOLLOWED BY ANY POSSIBLE SYMBOLISM.

DESCRIBE THE SETTING OR LOCATION FOR THE DREAM. THIS CAN INCLUDE TONE OR COLORING.
(EX. THE SETTING WAS HAPPY AND COLORFUL, DREARY AND BLACK AND WHITE, OR CAST IN SEPIA TONES.) WHAT MIGHT THE SETTING SYMBOLIZE?

ASK GOD TO GIVE YOU A SCRIPTURE TO ANCHOR THE DREAM, AND WRITE BELOW.
(NUMBERS, ESPECIALLY, CAN OFTEN BE CONNECTED TO A SCRIPTURE REFERENCE.)

RECORD ANY OTHER NOTES, PRAYER POINTS OR REVELATION ABOUT YOUR DREAM BELOW.

WRITE YOUR INTERPRETATION BELOW.

RECURRING SCENES OR SYMBOLS ARE IMPORTANT. CONSIDER ANY RECURRING THEMES OR SYMBOLS IN YOUR DREAMS. WHAT PATTERNS DO YOU NOTICE, AND WHAT MIGHT GOD BE COMMUNICATING THROUGH THEM?

REFLECT ON A DREAM THAT LEFT YOU FEELING AT PEACE. WHAT MESSAGE OF COMFORT OR ASSURANCE MIGHT GOD BE GIVING YOU?

Jan | Feb | Mar | Apr | May | Jun | Jul | Aug | Sep | Oct | Nov | Dec

1 2 3 4 5 6 7 8 9 10 11 12 13 14 15 16 17 18 19 20 21 22 23 24 25 26 27 28 29 30 31

WRITE OUT THE ENTIRE DREAM BELOW

HOW DID YOU FEEL DURING THE DREAM, AND AFTER YOU WOKE UP?

DESCRIBE YOUR POV IN THE DREAM? (EX. ARE YOU WATCHING FROM THE OUTSIDE? OR AN ACTIVE PARTICIPANT?)

LIST ANY THEMES FROM YOUR DREAM THAT YOU MAY HAVE SEEN POP UP BEFORE - IN LIFE, OR IN A PREVIOUS DREAM. WHAT MIGHT THESE THEMES REPRESENT?

Title Your Dream: ______________________________

LIST ANY COLORS, NUMBERS, OBJECTS, NAMES OR PEOPLE FROM THE DREAM, FOLLOWED BY ANY POSSIBLE SYMBOLISM.

DESCRIBE THE SETTING OR LOCATION FOR THE DREAM. THIS CAN INCLUDE TONE OR COLORING.
(EX. THE SETTING WAS HAPPY AND COLORFUL, DREARY AND BLACK AND WHITE, OR CAST IN SEPIA TONES.) WHAT MIGHT THE SETTING SYMBOLIZE?

ASK GOD TO GIVE YOU A SCRIPTURE TO ANCHOR THE DREAM, AND WRITE BELOW.
(NUMBERS, ESPECIALLY, CAN OFTEN BE CONNECTED TO A SCRIPTURE REFERENCE.)

RECORD ANY OTHER NOTES, PRAYER POINTS OR REVELATION ABOUT YOUR DREAM BELOW.

WRITE YOUR INTERPRETATION BELOW.

Jan | Feb | Mar | Apr | May | Jun | Jul | Aug | Sep | Oct | Nov | Dec

1 2 3 4 5 6 7 8 9 10 11 12 13 14 15 16 17 18 19 20 21 22 23 24 25 26 27 28 29 30 31

WRITE OUT THE ENTIRE DREAM BELOW

HOW DID YOU FEEL DURING THE DREAM, AND AFTER YOU WOKE UP?

DESCRIBE YOUR POV IN THE DREAM? (EX. ARE YOU WATCHING FROM THE OUTSIDE? OR AN ACTIVE PARTICIPANT?)

LIST ANY THEMES FROM YOUR DREAM THAT YOU MAY HAVE SEEN POP UP BEFORE - IN LIFE, OR IN A PREVIOUS DREAM. WHAT MIGHT THESE THEMES REPRESENT?

Title Your Dream: ______________________________

LIST ANY COLORS, NUMBERS, OBJECTS, NAMES OR PEOPLE FROM THE DREAM, FOLLOWED BY ANY POSSIBLE SYMBOLISM.

DESCRIBE THE SETTING OR LOCATION FOR THE DREAM. THIS CAN INCLUDE TONE OR COLORING.
(EX. THE SETTING WAS HAPPY AND COLORFUL, DREARY AND BLACK AND WHITE, OR CAST IN SEPIA TONES.) WHAT MIGHT THE SETTING SYMBOLIZE?

ASK GOD TO GIVE YOU A SCRIPTURE TO ANCHOR THE DREAM, AND WRITE BELOW.
(NUMBERS, ESPECIALLY, CAN OFTEN BE CONNECTED TO A SCRIPTURE REFERENCE.)

RECORD ANY OTHER NOTES, PRAYER POINTS OR REVELATION ABOUT YOUR DREAM BELOW.

WRITE YOUR INTERPRETATION BELOW.

Jan | Feb | Mar | Apr | May | Jun | Jul | Aug | Sep | Oct | Nov | Dec

1 2 3 4 5 6 7 8 9 10 11 12 13 14 15 16 17 18 19 20 21 22 23 24 25 26 27 28 29 30 31

WRITE OUT THE ENTIRE DREAM BELOW

HOW DID YOU FEEL DURING THE DREAM, AND AFTER YOU WOKE UP?

DESCRIBE YOUR POV IN THE DREAM? (EX. ARE YOU WATCHING FROM THE OUTSIDE? OR AN ACTIVE PARTICIPANT?)

LIST ANY THEMES FROM YOUR DREAM THAT YOU MAY HAVE SEEN POP UP BEFORE - IN LIFE, OR IN A PREVIOUS DREAM. WHAT MIGHT THESE THEMES REPRESENT?

Title Your Dream: ______________________________

LIST ANY COLORS, NUMBERS, OBJECTS, NAMES OR PEOPLE FROM THE DREAM, FOLLOWED BY ANY POSSIBLE SYMBOLISM.

DESCRIBE THE SETTING OR LOCATION FOR THE DREAM. THIS CAN INCLUDE TONE OR COLORING.
(EX. THE SETTING WAS HAPPY AND COLORFUL, DREARY AND BLACK AND WHITE, OR CAST IN SEPIA TONES.) WHAT MIGHT THE SETTING SYMBOLIZE?

ASK GOD TO GIVE YOU A SCRIPTURE TO ANCHOR THE DREAM, AND WRITE BELOW.
(NUMBERS, ESPECIALLY, CAN OFTEN BE CONNECTED TO A SCRIPTURE REFERENCE.)

RECORD ANY OTHER NOTES, PRAYER POINTS OR REVELATION ABOUT YOUR DREAM BELOW.

WRITE YOUR INTERPRETATION BELOW.

Jan | Feb | Mar | Apr | May | Jun | Jul | Aug | Sep | Oct | Nov | Dec

1 2 3 4 5 6 7 8 9 10 11 12 13 14 15 16 17 18 19 20 21 22 23 24 25 26 27 28 29 30 31

WRITE OUT THE ENTIRE DREAM BELOW

HOW DID YOU FEEL DURING THE DREAM, AND AFTER YOU WOKE UP?

DESCRIBE YOUR POV IN THE DREAM? (EX. ARE YOU WATCHING FROM THE OUTSIDE? OR AN ACTIVE PARTICIPANT?)

LIST ANY THEMES FROM YOUR DREAM THAT YOU MAY HAVE SEEN POP UP BEFORE - IN LIFE, OR IN A PREVIOUS DREAM. WHAT MIGHT THESE THEMES REPRESENT?

Title Your Dream: ____________________

LIST ANY COLORS, NUMBERS, OBJECTS, NAMES OR PEOPLE FROM THE DREAM, FOLLOWED BY ANY POSSIBLE SYMBOLISM.

DESCRIBE THE SETTING OR LOCATION FOR THE DREAM. THIS CAN INCLUDE TONE OR COLORING.
(EX. THE SETTING WAS HAPPY AND COLORFUL, DREARY AND BLACK AND WHITE, OR CAST IN SEPIA TONES.) WHAT MIGHT THE SETTING SYMBOLIZE?

ASK GOD TO GIVE YOU A SCRIPTURE TO ANCHOR THE DREAM, AND WRITE BELOW.
(NUMBERS, ESPECIALLY, CAN OFTEN BE CONNECTED TO A SCRIPTURE REFERENCE.)

RECORD ANY OTHER NOTES, PRAYER POINTS OR REVELATION ABOUT YOUR DREAM BELOW.

WRITE YOUR INTERPRETATION BELOW.

Jan | Feb | Mar | Apr | May | Jun | Jul | Aug | Sep | Oct | Nov | Dec

1 2 3 4 5 6 7 8 9 10 11 12 13 14 15 16 17 18 19 20 21 22 23 24 25 26 27 28 29 30 31

WRITE OUT THE ENTIRE DREAM BELOW

HOW DID YOU FEEL DURING THE DREAM, AND AFTER YOU WOKE UP?

DESCRIBE YOUR POV IN THE DREAM? (EX. ARE YOU WATCHING FROM THE OUTSIDE? OR AN ACTIVE PARTICIPANT?)

LIST ANY THEMES FROM YOUR DREAM THAT YOU MAY HAVE SEEN POP UP BEFORE - IN LIFE, OR IN A PREVIOUS DREAM. WHAT MIGHT THESE THEMES REPRESENT?

Title Your Dream: ______________________________

LIST ANY COLORS, NUMBERS, OBJECTS, NAMES OR PEOPLE FROM THE DREAM, FOLLOWED BY ANY POSSIBLE SYMBOLISM.

DESCRIBE THE SETTING OR LOCATION FOR THE DREAM. THIS CAN INCLUDE TONE OR COLORING.
(EX. THE SETTING WAS HAPPY AND COLORFUL, DREARY AND BLACK AND WHITE, OR CAST IN SEPIA TONES.) WHAT MIGHT THE SETTING SYMBOLIZE?

ASK GOD TO GIVE YOU A SCRIPTURE TO ANCHOR THE DREAM, AND WRITE BELOW.
(NUMBERS, ESPECIALLY, CAN OFTEN BE CONNECTED TO A SCRIPTURE REFERENCE.)

RECORD ANY OTHER NOTES, PRAYER POINTS OR REVELATION ABOUT YOUR DREAM BELOW.

WRITE YOUR INTERPRETATION BELOW.

DESCRIBE A DREAM THAT FELT PARTICULARLY CONFUSING OR UNSETTLING. ASK GOD FOR CLARITY AND WISDOM IN INTERPRETING THE CONFUSING MOMENTS, AND WRITE WHAT YOU THINK HE IS SHOWING YOU.

ASK GOD FOR A SCRIPTURE VERSE TO TIE TO YOUR DREAM. HOW DOES IT RELATE TO YOUR DREAM'S MESSAGE, AND HOW MIGHT GOD BE SPEAKING TO YOU ABOUT YOUR WAKING LIFE THROUGH THIS VERSE?

Jan | Feb | Mar | Apr | May | Jun | Jul | Aug | Sep | Oct | Nov | Dec

1 2 3 4 5 6 7 8 9 10 11 12 13 14 15 16 17 18 19 20 21 22 23 24 25 26 27 28 29 30 31

WRITE OUT THE ENTIRE DREAM BELOW

HOW DID YOU FEEL DURING THE DREAM, AND AFTER YOU WOKE UP?

DESCRIBE YOUR POV IN THE DREAM? (EX. ARE YOU WATCHING FROM THE OUTSIDE? OR AN ACTIVE PARTICIPANT?)

LIST ANY THEMES FROM YOUR DREAM THAT YOU MAY HAVE SEEN POP UP BEFORE - IN LIFE, OR IN A PREVIOUS DREAM. WHAT MIGHT THESE THEMES REPRESENT?

Title Your Dream: ______________________________

LIST ANY COLORS, NUMBERS, OBJECTS, NAMES OR PEOPLE FROM THE DREAM, FOLLOWED BY ANY POSSIBLE SYMBOLISM.

DESCRIBE THE SETTING OR LOCATION FOR THE DREAM. THIS CAN INCLUDE TONE OR COLORING.
(EX. THE SETTING WAS HAPPY AND COLORFUL, DREARY AND BLACK AND WHITE, OR CAST IN SEPIA TONES.) WHAT MIGHT THE SETTING SYMBOLIZE?

ASK GOD TO GIVE YOU A SCRIPTURE TO ANCHOR THE DREAM, AND WRITE BELOW.
(NUMBERS, ESPECIALLY, CAN OFTEN BE CONNECTED TO A SCRIPTURE REFERENCE.)

RECORD ANY OTHER NOTES, PRAYER POINTS OR REVELATION ABOUT YOUR DREAM BELOW.

WRITE YOUR INTERPRETATION BELOW.

Jan | Feb | Mar | Apr | May | Jun | Jul | Aug | Sep | Oct | Nov | Dec

1 2 3 4 5 6 7 8 9 10 11 12 13 14 15 16 17 18 19 20 21 22 23 24 25 26 27 28 29 30 31

WRITE OUT THE ENTIRE DREAM BELOW

HOW DID YOU FEEL DURING THE DREAM, AND AFTER YOU WOKE UP?

DESCRIBE YOUR POV IN THE DREAM? (EX. ARE YOU WATCHING FROM THE OUTSIDE? OR AN ACTIVE PARTICIPANT?)

LIST ANY THEMES FROM YOUR DREAM THAT YOU MAY HAVE SEEN POP UP BEFORE - IN LIFE, OR IN A PREVIOUS DREAM. WHAT MIGHT THESE THEMES REPRESENT?

Title Your Dream: ________________________________

LIST ANY COLORS, NUMBERS, OBJECTS, NAMES OR PEOPLE FROM THE DREAM, FOLLOWED BY ANY POSSIBLE SYMBOLISM.

DESCRIBE THE SETTING OR LOCATION FOR THE DREAM. THIS CAN INCLUDE TONE OR COLORING.
(EX. THE SETTING WAS HAPPY AND COLORFUL, DREARY AND BLACK AND WHITE, OR CAST IN SEPIA TONES.) WHAT MIGHT THE SETTING SYMBOLIZE?

ASK GOD TO GIVE YOU A SCRIPTURE TO ANCHOR THE DREAM, AND WRITE BELOW.
(NUMBERS, ESPECIALLY, CAN OFTEN BE CONNECTED TO A SCRIPTURE REFERENCE.)

RECORD ANY OTHER NOTES, PRAYER POINTS OR REVELATION ABOUT YOUR DREAM BELOW.

WRITE YOUR INTERPRETATION BELOW.

Jan | Feb | Mar | Apr | May | Jun | Jul | Aug | Sep | Oct | Nov | Dec

1 2 3 4 5 6 7 8 9 10 11 12 13 14 15 16 17 18 19 20 21 22 23 24 25 26 27 28 29 30 31

WRITE OUT THE ENTIRE DREAM BELOW

HOW DID YOU FEEL DURING THE DREAM, AND AFTER YOU WOKE UP?

DESCRIBE YOUR POV IN THE DREAM? (EX. ARE YOU WATCHING FROM THE OUTSIDE? OR AN ACTIVE PARTICIPANT?)

LIST ANY THEMES FROM YOUR DREAM THAT YOU MAY HAVE SEEN POP UP BEFORE - IN LIFE, OR IN A PREVIOUS DREAM. WHAT MIGHT THESE THEMES REPRESENT?

Title Your Dream: ______________________

LIST ANY COLORS, NUMBERS, OBJECTS, NAMES OR PEOPLE FROM THE DREAM, FOLLOWED BY ANY POSSIBLE SYMBOLISM.

DESCRIBE THE SETTING OR LOCATION FOR THE DREAM. THIS CAN INCLUDE TONE OR COLORING.
(EX. THE SETTING WAS HAPPY AND COLORFUL, DREARY AND BLACK AND WHITE, OR CAST IN SEPIA TONES.) WHAT MIGHT THE SETTING SYMBOLIZE?

ASK GOD TO GIVE YOU A SCRIPTURE TO ANCHOR THE DREAM, AND WRITE BELOW.
(NUMBERS, ESPECIALLY, CAN OFTEN BE CONNECTED TO A SCRIPTURE REFERENCE.)

RECORD ANY OTHER NOTES, PRAYER POINTS OR REVELATION ABOUT YOUR DREAM BELOW.

WRITE YOUR INTERPRETATION BELOW.

Jan | Feb | Mar | Apr | May | Jun | Jul | Aug | Sep | Oct | Nov | Dec

1 2 3 4 5 6 7 8 9 10 11 12 13 14 15 16 17 18 19 20 21 22 23 24 25 26 27 28 29 30 31

WRITE OUT THE ENTIRE DREAM BELOW

HOW DID YOU FEEL DURING THE DREAM, AND AFTER YOU WOKE UP?

DESCRIBE YOUR POV IN THE DREAM? (EX. ARE YOU WATCHING FROM THE OUTSIDE? OR AN ACTIVE PARTICIPANT?)

LIST ANY THEMES FROM YOUR DREAM THAT YOU MAY HAVE SEEN POP UP BEFORE - IN LIFE, OR IN A PREVIOUS DREAM. WHAT MIGHT THESE THEMES REPRESENT?

Title Your Dream: ___

LIST ANY COLORS, NUMBERS, OBJECTS, NAMES OR PEOPLE FROM THE DREAM, FOLLOWED BY ANY POSSIBLE SYMBOLISM.

DESCRIBE THE SETTING OR LOCATION FOR THE DREAM. THIS CAN INCLUDE TONE OR COLORING.
(EX. THE SETTING WAS HAPPY AND COLORFUL, DREARY AND BLACK AND WHITE, OR CAST IN SEPIA TONES.) WHAT MIGHT THE SETTING SYMBOLIZE?

ASK GOD TO GIVE YOU A SCRIPTURE TO ANCHOR THE DREAM, AND WRITE BELOW.
(NUMBERS, ESPECIALLY, CAN OFTEN BE CONNECTED TO A SCRIPTURE REFERENCE.)

RECORD ANY OTHER NOTES, PRAYER POINTS OR REVELATION ABOUT YOUR DREAM BELOW.

WRITE YOUR INTERPRETATION BELOW.

Jan | Feb | Mar | Apr | May | Jun | Jul | Aug | Sep | Oct | Nov | Dec

1 2 3 4 5 6 7 8 9 10 11 12 13 14 15 16 17 18 19 20 21 22 23 24 25 26 27 28 29 30 31

WRITE OUT THE ENTIRE DREAM BELOW

HOW DID YOU FEEL DURING THE DREAM, AND AFTER YOU WOKE UP?

DESCRIBE YOUR POV IN THE DREAM? (EX. ARE YOU WATCHING FROM THE OUTSIDE? OR AN ACTIVE PARTICIPANT?)

LIST ANY THEMES FROM YOUR DREAM THAT YOU MAY HAVE SEEN POP UP BEFORE - IN LIFE, OR IN A PREVIOUS DREAM. WHAT MIGHT THESE THEMES REPRESENT?

Title Your Dream: ________________________________

LIST ANY COLORS, NUMBERS, OBJECTS, NAMES OR PEOPLE FROM THE DREAM, FOLLOWED BY ANY POSSIBLE SYMBOLISM.

DESCRIBE THE SETTING OR LOCATION FOR THE DREAM. THIS CAN INCLUDE TONE OR COLORING.
(EX. THE SETTING WAS HAPPY AND COLORFUL, DREARY AND BLACK AND WHITE, OR CAST IN SEPIA TONES.) WHAT MIGHT THE SETTING SYMBOLIZE?

ASK GOD TO GIVE YOU A SCRIPTURE TO ANCHOR THE DREAM, AND WRITE BELOW.
(NUMBERS, ESPECIALLY, CAN OFTEN BE CONNECTED TO A SCRIPTURE REFERENCE.)

RECORD ANY OTHER NOTES, PRAYER POINTS OR REVELATION ABOUT YOUR DREAM BELOW.

WRITE YOUR INTERPRETATION BELOW.

REFLECT ON HOW YOUR DREAMS ARE ALIGNING WITH GOD'S PROMISES AND TEACHINGS. WHAT ENCOURAGEMENT OR DIRECTION MIGHT HE BE OFFERING YOU?

CONSIDER HOW YOUR DREAMS MIGHT BE CALLING YOU TO GROW SPIRITUALLY. WRITE DOWN ANY SPECIFIC AREAS OF GROWTH THAT YOU PERCEIVE. WHAT STEPS CAN YOU TAKE TO RESPOND TO THIS CALL IN YOUR DAILY LIFE?

Jan | Feb | Mar | Apr | May | Jun | Jul | Aug | Sep | Oct | Nov | Dec

1 2 3 4 5 6 7 8 9 10 11 12 13 14 15 16 17 18 19 20 21 22 23 24 25 26 27 28 29 30 31

WRITE OUT THE ENTIRE DREAM BELOW

HOW DID YOU FEEL DURING THE DREAM, AND AFTER YOU WOKE UP?

DESCRIBE YOUR POV IN THE DREAM? (EX. ARE YOU WATCHING FROM THE OUTSIDE? OR AN ACTIVE PARTICIPANT?)

LIST ANY THEMES FROM YOUR DREAM THAT YOU MAY HAVE SEEN POP UP BEFORE - IN LIFE, OR IN A PREVIOUS DREAM. WHAT MIGHT THESE THEMES REPRESENT?

Title Your Dream: ______

LIST ANY COLORS, NUMBERS, OBJECTS, NAMES OR PEOPLE FROM THE DREAM, FOLLOWED BY ANY POSSIBLE SYMBOLISM.

DESCRIBE THE SETTING OR LOCATION FOR THE DREAM. THIS CAN INCLUDE TONE OR COLORING.
(EX. THE SETTING WAS HAPPY AND COLORFUL, DREARY AND BLACK AND WHITE, OR CAST IN SEPIA TONES.) WHAT MIGHT THE SETTING SYMBOLIZE?

ASK GOD TO GIVE YOU A SCRIPTURE TO ANCHOR THE DREAM, AND WRITE BELOW.
(NUMBERS, ESPECIALLY, CAN OFTEN BE CONNECTED TO A SCRIPTURE REFERENCE.)

RECORD ANY OTHER NOTES, PRAYER POINTS OR REVELATION ABOUT YOUR DREAM BELOW.

WRITE YOUR INTERPRETATION BELOW.

Jan | Feb | Mar | Apr | May | Jun | Jul | Aug | Sep | Oct | Nov | Dec

1 2 3 4 5 6 7 8 9 10 11 12 13 14 15 16 17 18 19 20 21 22 23 24 25 26 27 28 29 30 31

WRITE OUT THE ENTIRE DREAM BELOW

HOW DID YOU FEEL DURING THE DREAM, AND AFTER YOU WOKE UP?

DESCRIBE YOUR POV IN THE DREAM? (EX. ARE YOU WATCHING FROM THE OUTSIDE? OR AN ACTIVE PARTICIPANT?)

LIST ANY THEMES FROM YOUR DREAM THAT YOU MAY HAVE SEEN POP UP BEFORE - IN LIFE, OR IN A PREVIOUS DREAM. WHAT MIGHT THESE THEMES REPRESENT?

Title Your Dream: ______________________

LIST ANY COLORS, NUMBERS, OBJECTS, NAMES OR PEOPLE FROM THE DREAM, FOLLOWED BY ANY POSSIBLE SYMBOLISM.

DESCRIBE THE SETTING OR LOCATION FOR THE DREAM. THIS CAN INCLUDE TONE OR COLORING.
(EX. THE SETTING WAS HAPPY AND COLORFUL, DREARY AND BLACK AND WHITE, OR CAST IN SEPIA TONES.) WHAT MIGHT THE SETTING SYMBOLIZE?

ASK GOD TO GIVE YOU A SCRIPTURE TO ANCHOR THE DREAM, AND WRITE BELOW.
(NUMBERS, ESPECIALLY, CAN OFTEN BE CONNECTED TO A SCRIPTURE REFERENCE.)

RECORD ANY OTHER NOTES, PRAYER POINTS OR REVELATION ABOUT YOUR DREAM BELOW.

WRITE YOUR INTERPRETATION BELOW.

Jan | Feb | Mar | Apr | May | Jun | Jul | Aug | Sep | Oct | Nov | Dec

1 2 3 4 5 6 7 8 9 10 11 12 13 14 15 16 17 18 19 20 21 22 23 24 25 26 27 28 29 30 31

WRITE OUT THE ENTIRE DREAM BELOW

HOW DID YOU FEEL DURING THE DREAM, AND AFTER YOU WOKE UP?

DESCRIBE YOUR POV IN THE DREAM? (EX. ARE YOU WATCHING FROM THE OUTSIDE? OR AN ACTIVE PARTICIPANT?)

LIST ANY THEMES FROM YOUR DREAM THAT YOU MAY HAVE SEEN POP UP BEFORE - IN LIFE, OR IN A PREVIOUS DREAM. WHAT MIGHT THESE THEMES REPRESENT?

Title Your Dream: ____________________

LIST ANY COLORS, NUMBERS, OBJECTS, NAMES OR PEOPLE FROM THE DREAM, FOLLOWED BY ANY POSSIBLE SYMBOLISM.

DESCRIBE THE SETTING OR LOCATION FOR THE DREAM. THIS CAN INCLUDE TONE OR COLORING.
(EX. THE SETTING WAS HAPPY AND COLORFUL, DREARY AND BLACK AND WHITE, OR CAST IN SEPIA TONES.) WHAT MIGHT THE SETTING SYMBOLIZE?

ASK GOD TO GIVE YOU A SCRIPTURE TO ANCHOR THE DREAM, AND WRITE BELOW.
(NUMBERS, ESPECIALLY, CAN OFTEN BE CONNECTED TO A SCRIPTURE REFERENCE.)

RECORD ANY OTHER NOTES, PRAYER POINTS OR REVELATION ABOUT YOUR DREAM BELOW.

WRITE YOUR INTERPRETATION BELOW.

Jan | Feb | Mar | Apr | May | Jun | Jul | Aug | Sep | Oct | Nov | Dec

1 2 3 4 5 6 7 8 9 10 11 12 13 14 15 16 17 18 19 20 21 22 23 24 25 26 27 28 29 30 31

WRITE OUT THE ENTIRE DREAM BELOW

HOW DID YOU FEEL DURING THE DREAM, AND AFTER YOU WOKE UP?

DESCRIBE YOUR POV IN THE DREAM? (EX. ARE YOU WATCHING FROM THE OUTSIDE? OR AN ACTIVE PARTICIPANT?)

LIST ANY THEMES FROM YOUR DREAM THAT YOU MAY HAVE SEEN POP UP BEFORE - IN LIFE, OR IN A PREVIOUS DREAM. WHAT MIGHT THESE THEMES REPRESENT?

Title Your Dream: ______________________________

LIST ANY COLORS, NUMBERS, OBJECTS, NAMES OR PEOPLE FROM THE DREAM, FOLLOWED BY ANY POSSIBLE SYMBOLISM.

DESCRIBE THE SETTING OR LOCATION FOR THE DREAM. THIS CAN INCLUDE TONE OR COLORING.
(EX. THE SETTING WAS HAPPY AND COLORFUL, DREARY AND BLACK AND WHITE, OR CAST IN SEPIA TONES.) WHAT MIGHT THE SETTING SYMBOLIZE?

ASK GOD TO GIVE YOU A SCRIPTURE TO ANCHOR THE DREAM, AND WRITE BELOW.
(NUMBERS, ESPECIALLY, CAN OFTEN BE CONNECTED TO A SCRIPTURE REFERENCE.)

RECORD ANY OTHER NOTES, PRAYER POINTS OR REVELATION ABOUT YOUR DREAM BELOW.

WRITE YOUR INTERPRETATION BELOW.

Jan | Feb | Mar | Apr | May | Jun | Jul | Aug | Sep | Oct | Nov | Dec

1 2 3 4 5 6 7 8 9 10 11 12 13 14 15 16 17 18 19 20 21 22 23 24 25 26 27 28 29 30 31

WRITE OUT THE ENTIRE DREAM BELOW

HOW DID YOU FEEL DURING THE DREAM, AND AFTER YOU WOKE UP?

DESCRIBE YOUR POV IN THE DREAM? (EX. ARE YOU WATCHING FROM THE OUTSIDE? OR AN ACTIVE PARTICIPANT?)

LIST ANY THEMES FROM YOUR DREAM THAT YOU MAY HAVE SEEN POP UP BEFORE - IN LIFE, OR IN A PREVIOUS DREAM. WHAT MIGHT THESE THEMES REPRESENT?

Title Your Dream: ______________________________

LIST ANY COLORS, NUMBERS, OBJECTS, NAMES OR PEOPLE FROM THE DREAM, FOLLOWED BY ANY POSSIBLE SYMBOLISM.

DESCRIBE THE SETTING OR LOCATION FOR THE DREAM. THIS CAN INCLUDE TONE OR COLORING.
(EX. THE SETTING WAS HAPPY AND COLORFUL, DREARY AND BLACK AND WHITE, OR CAST IN SEPIA TONES.) WHAT MIGHT THE SETTING SYMBOLIZE?

ASK GOD TO GIVE YOU A SCRIPTURE TO ANCHOR THE DREAM, AND WRITE BELOW.
(NUMBERS, ESPECIALLY, CAN OFTEN BE CONNECTED TO A SCRIPTURE REFERENCE.)

RECORD ANY OTHER NOTES, PRAYER POINTS OR REVELATION ABOUT YOUR DREAM BELOW.

WRITE YOUR INTERPRETATION BELOW.

OFTEN, JESUS, GOD, AND THE HOLY SPIRIT CAN APPEAR IN OUR DREAMS SYMBOLICALLY THROUGH OTHER PEOPLE. FOR EXAMPLE, SOMEONE NAMED CHRIS MIGHT SYMBOLIZE CHRIST; YOUR NATURAL FATHER MIGHT APPEAR SYMBOLIZING YOUR HEAVENLY FATHER; A COUNSELOR, DOCTOR, TEACHER, OR POLICE OFFICER MIGHT SYMBOLIZE THE HOLY SPIRIT, WHO WAS SENT AS OUR HELPER. REFLECT ON ANY SYMBOLIC REPRESENTATIONS OF THE FATHER, SON, AND HOLY SPIRIT THAT HAVE APPEARED IN YOUR DREAM LIFE. WHAT DO YOU THINK GOD IS SHOWING YOU ABOUT HIS NATURE?

HAVE YOU NOTICED ANY SYMBOLISM FROM YOUR DREAMS THAT MIGHT POINT TO A WOUND FROM YOUR PAST THAT GOD WANTS TO HEAL?

Jan | Feb | Mar | Apr | May | Jun | Jul | Aug | Sep | Oct | Nov | Dec

1 2 3 4 5 6 7 8 9 10 11 12 13 14 15 16 17 18 19 20 21 22 23 24 25 26 27 28 29 30 31

WRITE OUT THE ENTIRE DREAM BELOW

HOW DID YOU FEEL DURING THE DREAM, AND AFTER YOU WOKE UP?

DESCRIBE YOUR POV IN THE DREAM? (EX. ARE YOU WATCHING FROM THE OUTSIDE? OR AN ACTIVE PARTICIPANT?)

LIST ANY THEMES FROM YOUR DREAM THAT YOU MAY HAVE SEEN POP UP BEFORE - IN LIFE, OR IN A PREVIOUS DREAM. WHAT MIGHT THESE THEMES REPRESENT?

Title Your Dream: ______________________________

LIST ANY COLORS, NUMBERS, OBJECTS, NAMES OR PEOPLE FROM THE DREAM, FOLLOWED BY ANY POSSIBLE SYMBOLISM.

DESCRIBE THE SETTING OR LOCATION FOR THE DREAM. THIS CAN INCLUDE TONE OR COLORING.
(EX. THE SETTING WAS HAPPY AND COLORFUL, DREARY AND BLACK AND WHITE, OR CAST IN SEPIA TONES.) WHAT MIGHT THE SETTING SYMBOLIZE?

ASK GOD TO GIVE YOU A SCRIPTURE TO ANCHOR THE DREAM, AND WRITE BELOW.
(NUMBERS, ESPECIALLY, CAN OFTEN BE CONNECTED TO A SCRIPTURE REFERENCE.)

RECORD ANY OTHER NOTES, PRAYER POINTS OR REVELATION ABOUT YOUR DREAM BELOW.

WRITE YOUR INTERPRETATION BELOW.

Jan | Feb | Mar | Apr | May | Jun | Jul | Aug | Sep | Oct | Nov | Dec

1 2 3 4 5 6 7 8 9 10 11 12 13 14 15 16 17 18 19 20 21 22 23 24 25 26 27 28 29 30 31

WRITE OUT THE ENTIRE DREAM BELOW

HOW DID YOU FEEL DURING THE DREAM, AND AFTER YOU WOKE UP?

DESCRIBE YOUR POV IN THE DREAM? (EX. ARE YOU WATCHING FROM THE OUTSIDE? OR AN ACTIVE PARTICIPANT?)

LIST ANY THEMES FROM YOUR DREAM THAT YOU MAY HAVE SEEN POP UP BEFORE - IN LIFE, OR IN A PREVIOUS DREAM. WHAT MIGHT THESE THEMES REPRESENT?

Title Your Dream: ______________________

LIST ANY COLORS, NUMBERS, OBJECTS, NAMES OR PEOPLE FROM THE DREAM, FOLLOWED BY ANY POSSIBLE SYMBOLISM.

DESCRIBE THE SETTING OR LOCATION FOR THE DREAM. THIS CAN INCLUDE TONE OR COLORING.
(EX. THE SETTING WAS HAPPY AND COLORFUL, DREARY AND BLACK AND WHITE, OR CAST IN SEPIA TONES.) WHAT MIGHT THE SETTING SYMBOLIZE?

ASK GOD TO GIVE YOU A SCRIPTURE TO ANCHOR THE DREAM, AND WRITE BELOW.
(NUMBERS, ESPECIALLY, CAN OFTEN BE CONNECTED TO A SCRIPTURE REFERENCE.)

RECORD ANY OTHER NOTES, PRAYER POINTS OR REVELATION ABOUT YOUR DREAM BELOW.

WRITE YOUR INTERPRETATION BELOW.

Jan | Feb | Mar | Apr | May | Jun | Jul | Aug | Sep | Oct | Nov | Dec

1 2 3 4 5 6 7 8 9 10 11 12 13 14 15 16 17 18 19 20 21 22 23 24 25 26 27 28 29 30 31

WRITE OUT THE ENTIRE DREAM BELOW

HOW DID YOU FEEL DURING THE DREAM, AND AFTER YOU WOKE UP?

DESCRIBE YOUR POV IN THE DREAM? (EX. ARE YOU WATCHING FROM THE OUTSIDE? OR AN ACTIVE PARTICIPANT?)

LIST ANY THEMES FROM YOUR DREAM THAT YOU MAY HAVE SEEN POP UP BEFORE - IN LIFE, OR IN A PREVIOUS DREAM. WHAT MIGHT THESE THEMES REPRESENT?

Title Your Dream: ____________________

LIST ANY COLORS, NUMBERS, OBJECTS, NAMES OR PEOPLE FROM THE DREAM, FOLLOWED BY ANY POSSIBLE SYMBOLISM.

DESCRIBE THE SETTING OR LOCATION FOR THE DREAM. THIS CAN INCLUDE TONE OR COLORING.
(EX. THE SETTING WAS HAPPY AND COLORFUL, DREARY AND BLACK AND WHITE, OR CAST IN SEPIA TONES.) WHAT MIGHT THE SETTING SYMBOLIZE?

ASK GOD TO GIVE YOU A SCRIPTURE TO ANCHOR THE DREAM, AND WRITE BELOW.
(NUMBERS, ESPECIALLY, CAN OFTEN BE CONNECTED TO A SCRIPTURE REFERENCE.)

RECORD ANY OTHER NOTES, PRAYER POINTS OR REVELATION ABOUT YOUR DREAM BELOW.

WRITE YOUR INTERPRETATION BELOW.

Jan | Feb | Mar | Apr | May | Jun | Jul | Aug | Sep | Oct | Nov | Dec

1 2 3 4 5 6 7 8 9 10 11 12 13 14 15 16 17 18 19 20 21 22 23 24 25 26 27 28 29 30 31

WRITE OUT THE ENTIRE DREAM BELOW

HOW DID YOU FEEL DURING THE DREAM, AND AFTER YOU WOKE UP?

DESCRIBE YOUR POV IN THE DREAM? (EX. ARE YOU WATCHING FROM THE OUTSIDE? OR AN ACTIVE PARTICIPANT?)

LIST ANY THEMES FROM YOUR DREAM THAT YOU MAY HAVE SEEN POP UP BEFORE - IN LIFE, OR IN A PREVIOUS DREAM. WHAT MIGHT THESE THEMES REPRESENT?

Title Your Dream: ______________________

LIST ANY COLORS, NUMBERS, OBJECTS, NAMES OR PEOPLE FROM THE DREAM, FOLLOWED BY ANY POSSIBLE SYMBOLISM.

DESCRIBE THE SETTING OR LOCATION FOR THE DREAM. THIS CAN INCLUDE TONE OR COLORING.
(EX. THE SETTING WAS HAPPY AND COLORFUL, DREARY AND BLACK AND WHITE, OR CAST IN SEPIA TONES.) WHAT MIGHT THE SETTING SYMBOLIZE?

ASK GOD TO GIVE YOU A SCRIPTURE TO ANCHOR THE DREAM, AND WRITE BELOW.
(NUMBERS, ESPECIALLY, CAN OFTEN BE CONNECTED TO A SCRIPTURE REFERENCE.)

RECORD ANY OTHER NOTES, PRAYER POINTS OR REVELATION ABOUT YOUR DREAM BELOW.

WRITE YOUR INTERPRETATION BELOW.

Jan | Feb | Mar | Apr | May | Jun | Jul | Aug | Sep | Oct | Nov | Dec

1 2 3 4 5 6 7 8 9 10 11 12 13 14 15 16 17 18 19 20 21 22 23 24 25 26 27 28 29 30 31

WRITE OUT THE ENTIRE DREAM BELOW

HOW DID YOU FEEL DURING THE DREAM, AND AFTER YOU WOKE UP?

DESCRIBE YOUR POV IN THE DREAM? (EX. ARE YOU WATCHING FROM THE OUTSIDE? OR AN ACTIVE PARTICIPANT?)

LIST ANY THEMES FROM YOUR DREAM THAT YOU MAY HAVE SEEN POP UP BEFORE - IN LIFE, OR IN A PREVIOUS DREAM. WHAT MIGHT THESE THEMES REPRESENT?

Title Your Dream: ______________________

LIST ANY COLORS, NUMBERS, OBJECTS, NAMES OR PEOPLE FROM THE DREAM, FOLLOWED BY ANY POSSIBLE SYMBOLISM.

DESCRIBE THE SETTING OR LOCATION FOR THE DREAM. THIS CAN INCLUDE TONE OR COLORING.
(EX. THE SETTING WAS HAPPY AND COLORFUL, DREARY AND BLACK AND WHITE, OR CAST IN SEPIA TONES.) WHAT MIGHT THE SETTING SYMBOLIZE?

ASK GOD TO GIVE YOU A SCRIPTURE TO ANCHOR THE DREAM, AND WRITE BELOW.
(NUMBERS, ESPECIALLY, CAN OFTEN BE CONNECTED TO A SCRIPTURE REFERENCE.)

RECORD ANY OTHER NOTES, PRAYER POINTS OR REVELATION ABOUT YOUR DREAM BELOW.

WRITE YOUR INTERPRETATION BELOW.

REFLECT ON A DREAM THAT MADE YOU FEEL AFRAID. WHAT SYMBOLIZED THE THREATS, ATTACKS, OR CIRCUMSTANCES THAT CAUSED YOUR FEAR? ASK THE LORD TO SHOW YOU WHAT THIS MIGHT REPRESENT IN YOUR LIFE.

CONSIDER THE PRESENCE OF NUMBERS IN YOUR DREAMS. WHAT IS THE SYMBOLISM ASSOCIATED WITH ANY NUMBERS, AND WHAT MIGHT THAT MEAN IN YOUR LIFE?

Jan | Feb | Mar | Apr | May | Jun | Jul | Aug | Sep | Oct | Nov | Dec

1 2 3 4 5 6 7 8 9 10 11 12 13 14 15 16 17 18 19 20 21 22 23 24 25 26 27 28 29 30 31

WRITE OUT THE ENTIRE DREAM BELOW

HOW DID YOU FEEL DURING THE DREAM, AND AFTER YOU WOKE UP?

DESCRIBE YOUR POV IN THE DREAM? (EX. ARE YOU WATCHING FROM THE OUTSIDE? OR AN ACTIVE PARTICIPANT?)

LIST ANY THEMES FROM YOUR DREAM THAT YOU MAY HAVE SEEN POP UP BEFORE - IN LIFE, OR IN A PREVIOUS DREAM. WHAT MIGHT THESE THEMES REPRESENT?

Title Your Dream: ______________________________

LIST ANY COLORS, NUMBERS, OBJECTS, NAMES OR PEOPLE FROM THE DREAM, FOLLOWED BY ANY POSSIBLE SYMBOLISM.

DESCRIBE THE SETTING OR LOCATION FOR THE DREAM. THIS CAN INCLUDE TONE OR COLORING.
(EX. THE SETTING WAS HAPPY AND COLORFUL, DREARY AND BLACK AND WHITE, OR CAST IN SEPIA TONES.) WHAT MIGHT THE SETTING SYMBOLIZE?

ASK GOD TO GIVE YOU A SCRIPTURE TO ANCHOR THE DREAM, AND WRITE BELOW.
(NUMBERS, ESPECIALLY, CAN OFTEN BE CONNECTED TO A SCRIPTURE REFERENCE.)

RECORD ANY OTHER NOTES, PRAYER POINTS OR REVELATION ABOUT YOUR DREAM BELOW.

WRITE YOUR INTERPRETATION BELOW.

Jan | Feb | Mar | Apr | May | Jun | Jul | Aug | Sep | Oct | Nov | Dec

1 2 3 4 5 6 7 8 9 10 11 12 13 14 15 16 17 18 19 20 21 22 23 24 25 26 27 28 29 30 31

WRITE OUT THE ENTIRE DREAM BELOW

HOW DID YOU FEEL DURING THE DREAM, AND AFTER YOU WOKE UP?

DESCRIBE YOUR POV IN THE DREAM? (EX. ARE YOU WATCHING FROM THE OUTSIDE? OR AN ACTIVE PARTICIPANT?)

LIST ANY THEMES FROM YOUR DREAM THAT YOU MAY HAVE SEEN POP UP BEFORE - IN LIFE, OR IN A PREVIOUS DREAM. WHAT MIGHT THESE THEMES REPRESENT?

Title Your Dream: ______________________________

LIST ANY COLORS, NUMBERS, OBJECTS, NAMES OR PEOPLE FROM THE DREAM, FOLLOWED BY ANY POSSIBLE SYMBOLISM.

DESCRIBE THE SETTING OR LOCATION FOR THE DREAM. THIS CAN INCLUDE TONE OR COLORING.
(EX. THE SETTING WAS HAPPY AND COLORFUL, DREARY AND BLACK AND WHITE, OR CAST IN SEPIA TONES.) WHAT MIGHT THE SETTING SYMBOLIZE?

ASK GOD TO GIVE YOU A SCRIPTURE TO ANCHOR THE DREAM, AND WRITE BELOW.
(NUMBERS, ESPECIALLY, CAN OFTEN BE CONNECTED TO A SCRIPTURE REFERENCE.)

RECORD ANY OTHER NOTES, PRAYER POINTS OR REVELATION ABOUT YOUR DREAM BELOW.

WRITE YOUR INTERPRETATION BELOW.

Jan | Feb | Mar | Apr | May | Jun | Jul | Aug | Sep | Oct | Nov | Dec

1 2 3 4 5 6 7 8 9 10 11 12 13 14 15 16 17 18 19 20 21 22 23 24 25 26 27 28 29 30 31

WRITE OUT THE ENTIRE DREAM BELOW

HOW DID YOU FEEL DURING THE DREAM, AND AFTER YOU WOKE UP?

DESCRIBE YOUR POV IN THE DREAM? (EX. ARE YOU WATCHING FROM THE OUTSIDE? OR AN ACTIVE PARTICIPANT?)

LIST ANY THEMES FROM YOUR DREAM THAT YOU MAY HAVE SEEN POP UP BEFORE - IN LIFE, OR IN A PREVIOUS DREAM. WHAT MIGHT THESE THEMES REPRESENT?

Title Your Dream: ____________________

LIST ANY COLORS, NUMBERS, OBJECTS, NAMES OR PEOPLE FROM THE DREAM, FOLLOWED BY ANY POSSIBLE SYMBOLISM.

DESCRIBE THE SETTING OR LOCATION FOR THE DREAM. THIS CAN INCLUDE TONE OR COLORING.
(EX. THE SETTING WAS HAPPY AND COLORFUL, DREARY AND BLACK AND WHITE, OR CAST IN SEPIA TONES.) WHAT MIGHT THE SETTING SYMBOLIZE?

ASK GOD TO GIVE YOU A SCRIPTURE TO ANCHOR THE DREAM, AND WRITE BELOW.
(NUMBERS, ESPECIALLY, CAN OFTEN BE CONNECTED TO A SCRIPTURE REFERENCE.)

RECORD ANY OTHER NOTES, PRAYER POINTS OR REVELATION ABOUT YOUR DREAM BELOW.

WRITE YOUR INTERPRETATION BELOW.

Jan | Feb | Mar | Apr | May | Jun | Jul | Aug | Sep | Oct | Nov | Dec

1 2 3 4 5 6 7 8 9 10 11 12 13 14 15 16 17 18 19 20 21 22 23 24 25 26 27 28 29 30 31

WRITE OUT THE ENTIRE DREAM BELOW

HOW DID YOU FEEL DURING THE DREAM, AND AFTER YOU WOKE UP?

DESCRIBE YOUR POV IN THE DREAM? (EX. ARE YOU WATCHING FROM THE OUTSIDE? OR AN ACTIVE PARTICIPANT?)

LIST ANY THEMES FROM YOUR DREAM THAT YOU MAY HAVE SEEN POP UP BEFORE - IN LIFE, OR IN A PREVIOUS DREAM. WHAT MIGHT THESE THEMES REPRESENT?

Title Your Dream: ____________________

LIST ANY COLORS, NUMBERS, OBJECTS, NAMES OR PEOPLE FROM THE DREAM, FOLLOWED BY ANY POSSIBLE SYMBOLISM.

DESCRIBE THE SETTING OR LOCATION FOR THE DREAM. THIS CAN INCLUDE TONE OR COLORING.
(EX. THE SETTING WAS HAPPY AND COLORFUL, DREARY AND BLACK AND WHITE, OR CAST IN SEPIA TONES.) WHAT MIGHT THE SETTING SYMBOLIZE?

ASK GOD TO GIVE YOU A SCRIPTURE TO ANCHOR THE DREAM, AND WRITE BELOW.
(NUMBERS, ESPECIALLY, CAN OFTEN BE CONNECTED TO A SCRIPTURE REFERENCE.)

RECORD ANY OTHER NOTES, PRAYER POINTS OR REVELATION ABOUT YOUR DREAM BELOW.

WRITE YOUR INTERPRETATION BELOW.

Jan | Feb | Mar | Apr | May | Jun | Jul | Aug | Sep | Oct | Nov | Dec

1 2 3 4 5 6 7 8 9 10 11 12 13 14 15 16 17 18 19 20 21 22 23 24 25 26 27 28 29 30 31

WRITE OUT THE ENTIRE DREAM BELOW

HOW DID YOU FEEL DURING THE DREAM, AND AFTER YOU WOKE UP?

DESCRIBE YOUR POV IN THE DREAM? (EX. ARE YOU WATCHING FROM THE OUTSIDE? OR AN ACTIVE PARTICIPANT?)

LIST ANY THEMES FROM YOUR DREAM THAT YOU MAY HAVE SEEN POP UP BEFORE - IN LIFE, OR IN A PREVIOUS DREAM. WHAT MIGHT THESE THEMES REPRESENT?

Title Your Dream: ______________________________

LIST ANY COLORS, NUMBERS, OBJECTS, NAMES OR PEOPLE FROM THE DREAM, FOLLOWED BY ANY POSSIBLE SYMBOLISM.

DESCRIBE THE SETTING OR LOCATION FOR THE DREAM. THIS CAN INCLUDE TONE OR COLORING.
(EX. THE SETTING WAS HAPPY AND COLORFUL, DREARY AND BLACK AND WHITE, OR CAST IN SEPIA TONES.) WHAT MIGHT THE SETTING SYMBOLIZE?

ASK GOD TO GIVE YOU A SCRIPTURE TO ANCHOR THE DREAM, AND WRITE BELOW.
(NUMBERS, ESPECIALLY, CAN OFTEN BE CONNECTED TO A SCRIPTURE REFERENCE.)

RECORD ANY OTHER NOTES, PRAYER POINTS OR REVELATION ABOUT YOUR DREAM BELOW.

WRITE YOUR INTERPRETATION BELOW.

HAVE YOU HAD ANY DREAMS THAT MIGHT BE RELEVANT TO YOUR OCCUPATION OR FUTURE CAREER PATH? WRITE ANY THEMES THAT ARISE AS YOU HAVE CONSIDERED THESE TOPICS AND PRAYED ABOUT THEM.

WHAT WARNINGS HAVE YOU EXPERIENCED IN DREAMS? HOW ARE YOU ACTIVELY PRAYING ABOUT THEM AND POSTURING YOUR HEART IN RESPONSE?

Jan | Feb | Mar | Apr | May | Jun | Jul | Aug | Sep | Oct | Nov | Dec

1 2 3 4 5 6 7 8 9 10 11 12 13 14 15 16 17 18 19 20 21 22 23 24 25 26 27 28 29 30 31

WRITE OUT THE ENTIRE DREAM BELOW

HOW DID YOU FEEL DURING THE DREAM, AND AFTER YOU WOKE UP?

DESCRIBE YOUR POV IN THE DREAM? (EX. ARE YOU WATCHING FROM THE OUTSIDE? OR AN ACTIVE PARTICIPANT?)

LIST ANY THEMES FROM YOUR DREAM THAT YOU MAY HAVE SEEN POP UP BEFORE - IN LIFE, OR IN A PREVIOUS DREAM. WHAT MIGHT THESE THEMES REPRESENT?

Title Your Dream: ______________________

LIST ANY COLORS, NUMBERS, OBJECTS, NAMES OR PEOPLE FROM THE DREAM, FOLLOWED BY ANY POSSIBLE SYMBOLISM.

DESCRIBE THE SETTING OR LOCATION FOR THE DREAM. THIS CAN INCLUDE TONE OR COLORING.
(EX. THE SETTING WAS HAPPY AND COLORFUL, DREARY AND BLACK AND WHITE, OR CAST IN SEPIA TONES.) WHAT MIGHT THE SETTING SYMBOLIZE?

ASK GOD TO GIVE YOU A SCRIPTURE TO ANCHOR THE DREAM, AND WRITE BELOW.
(NUMBERS, ESPECIALLY, CAN OFTEN BE CONNECTED TO A SCRIPTURE REFERENCE.)

RECORD ANY OTHER NOTES, PRAYER POINTS OR REVELATION ABOUT YOUR DREAM BELOW.

WRITE YOUR INTERPRETATION BELOW.

Jan | Feb | Mar | Apr | May | Jun | Jul | Aug | Sep | Oct | Nov | Dec

1 2 3 4 5 6 7 8 9 10 11 12 13 14 15 16 17 18 19 20 21 22 23 24 25 26 27 28 29 30 31

WRITE OUT THE ENTIRE DREAM BELOW

HOW DID YOU FEEL DURING THE DREAM, AND AFTER YOU WOKE UP?

DESCRIBE YOUR POV IN THE DREAM? (EX. ARE YOU WATCHING FROM THE OUTSIDE? OR AN ACTIVE PARTICIPANT?)

LIST ANY THEMES FROM YOUR DREAM THAT YOU MAY HAVE SEEN POP UP BEFORE - IN LIFE, OR IN A PREVIOUS DREAM. WHAT MIGHT THESE THEMES REPRESENT?

Title Your Dream: ______________________

LIST ANY COLORS, NUMBERS, OBJECTS, NAMES OR PEOPLE FROM THE DREAM, FOLLOWED BY ANY POSSIBLE SYMBOLISM.

DESCRIBE THE SETTING OR LOCATION FOR THE DREAM. THIS CAN INCLUDE TONE OR COLORING.
(EX. THE SETTING WAS HAPPY AND COLORFUL, DREARY AND BLACK AND WHITE, OR CAST IN SEPIA TONES.) WHAT MIGHT THE SETTING SYMBOLIZE?

ASK GOD TO GIVE YOU A SCRIPTURE TO ANCHOR THE DREAM, AND WRITE BELOW.
(NUMBERS, ESPECIALLY, CAN OFTEN BE CONNECTED TO A SCRIPTURE REFERENCE.)

RECORD ANY OTHER NOTES, PRAYER POINTS OR REVELATION ABOUT YOUR DREAM BELOW.

WRITE YOUR INTERPRETATION BELOW.

Jan | Feb | Mar | Apr | May | Jun | Jul | Aug | Sep | Oct | Nov | Dec

1 2 3 4 5 6 7 8 9 10 11 12 13 14 15 16 17 18 19 20 21 22 23 24 25 26 27 28 29 30 31

WRITE OUT THE ENTIRE DREAM BELOW

HOW DID YOU FEEL DURING THE DREAM, AND AFTER YOU WOKE UP?

DESCRIBE YOUR POV IN THE DREAM? (EX. ARE YOU WATCHING FROM THE OUTSIDE? OR AN ACTIVE PARTICIPANT?)

LIST ANY THEMES FROM YOUR DREAM THAT YOU MAY HAVE SEEN POP UP BEFORE - IN LIFE, OR IN A PREVIOUS DREAM. WHAT MIGHT THESE THEMES REPRESENT?

Title Your Dream: ______________________________

LIST ANY COLORS, NUMBERS, OBJECTS, NAMES OR PEOPLE FROM THE DREAM, FOLLOWED BY ANY POSSIBLE SYMBOLISM.

DESCRIBE THE SETTING OR LOCATION FOR THE DREAM. THIS CAN INCLUDE TONE OR COLORING.
(EX. THE SETTING WAS HAPPY AND COLORFUL, DREARY AND BLACK AND WHITE, OR CAST IN SEPIA TONES.) WHAT MIGHT THE SETTING SYMBOLIZE?

ASK GOD TO GIVE YOU A SCRIPTURE TO ANCHOR THE DREAM, AND WRITE BELOW.
(NUMBERS, ESPECIALLY, CAN OFTEN BE CONNECTED TO A SCRIPTURE REFERENCE.)

RECORD ANY OTHER NOTES, PRAYER POINTS OR REVELATION ABOUT YOUR DREAM BELOW.

WRITE YOUR INTERPRETATION BELOW.

Jan | Feb | Mar | Apr | May | Jun | Jul | Aug | Sep | Oct | Nov | Dec

1 2 3 4 5 6 7 8 9 10 11 12 13 14 15 16 17 18 19 20 21 22 23 24 25 26 27 28 29 30 31

WRITE OUT THE ENTIRE DREAM BELOW

HOW DID YOU FEEL DURING THE DREAM, AND AFTER YOU WOKE UP?

DESCRIBE YOUR POV IN THE DREAM? (EX. ARE YOU WATCHING FROM THE OUTSIDE? OR AN ACTIVE PARTICIPANT?)

LIST ANY THEMES FROM YOUR DREAM THAT YOU MAY HAVE SEEN POP UP BEFORE - IN LIFE, OR IN A PREVIOUS DREAM. WHAT MIGHT THESE THEMES REPRESENT?

Title Your Dream: ____________________

LIST ANY COLORS, NUMBERS, OBJECTS, NAMES OR PEOPLE FROM THE DREAM, FOLLOWED BY ANY POSSIBLE SYMBOLISM.

DESCRIBE THE SETTING OR LOCATION FOR THE DREAM. THIS CAN INCLUDE TONE OR COLORING.
(EX. THE SETTING WAS HAPPY AND COLORFUL, DREARY AND BLACK AND WHITE, OR CAST IN SEPIA TONES.) WHAT MIGHT THE SETTING SYMBOLIZE?

ASK GOD TO GIVE YOU A SCRIPTURE TO ANCHOR THE DREAM, AND WRITE BELOW.
(NUMBERS, ESPECIALLY, CAN OFTEN BE CONNECTED TO A SCRIPTURE REFERENCE.)

RECORD ANY OTHER NOTES, PRAYER POINTS OR REVELATION ABOUT YOUR DREAM BELOW.

WRITE YOUR INTERPRETATION BELOW.

Jan | Feb | Mar | Apr | May | Jun | Jul | Aug | Sep | Oct | Nov | Dec

1 2 3 4 5 6 7 8 9 10 11 12 13 14 15 16 17 18 19 20 21 22 23 24 25 26 27 28 29 30 31

WRITE OUT THE ENTIRE DREAM BELOW

HOW DID YOU FEEL DURING THE DREAM, AND AFTER YOU WOKE UP?

DESCRIBE YOUR POV IN THE DREAM? (EX. ARE YOU WATCHING FROM THE OUTSIDE? OR AN ACTIVE PARTICIPANT?)

LIST ANY THEMES FROM YOUR DREAM THAT YOU MAY HAVE SEEN POP UP BEFORE - IN LIFE, OR IN A PREVIOUS DREAM. WHAT MIGHT THESE THEMES REPRESENT?

Title Your Dream: ______________________

LIST ANY COLORS, NUMBERS, OBJECTS, NAMES OR PEOPLE FROM THE DREAM, FOLLOWED BY ANY POSSIBLE SYMBOLISM.

DESCRIBE THE SETTING OR LOCATION FOR THE DREAM. THIS CAN INCLUDE TONE OR COLORING.
(EX. THE SETTING WAS HAPPY AND COLORFUL, DREARY AND BLACK AND WHITE, OR CAST IN SEPIA TONES.) WHAT MIGHT THE SETTING SYMBOLIZE?

ASK GOD TO GIVE YOU A SCRIPTURE TO ANCHOR THE DREAM, AND WRITE BELOW.
(NUMBERS, ESPECIALLY, CAN OFTEN BE CONNECTED TO A SCRIPTURE REFERENCE.)

RECORD ANY OTHER NOTES, PRAYER POINTS OR REVELATION ABOUT YOUR DREAM BELOW.

WRITE YOUR INTERPRETATION BELOW.

PRAYERS

A PRAYER FOR PEACEFUL SLEEP

Heavenly Father,

As I lie down to sleep, I pray for an awareness of Your peace and comfort surrounding me. Help me to cast all my cares and anxieties on You, knowing that You care for me, as Your Word says in 1 Peter 5:7. I ask You to quiet my mind and calm my heart so that I may rest in the assurance of Your love and protection.

Fill my mind and spirit with Your truth so that I may rest in the knowledge of Your goodness and faithfulness. I pray that You will surround me with Your angels, who are encamped around those who fear You, according to Psalm 34:7. Protect me from all harm and danger and keep me safe through the night.

I bind every spirit of fear that would seek to torment me in the night and declare Psalm 4:8 over me and my household: *"In peace I will lie down and sleep, for you alone, Lord, make me dwell in safety"* (NIV).

Thank You for the gift of sleep and for the refreshment and renewal it brings to my body and soul. I trust in You, and I know that You will keep me in perfect peace as my mind is stayed on You, as it says in Isaiah 26:3.

In Jesus's name I pray, amen.

A PRAYER FOR THE ACTIVATION OF DREAMS

Lord,

I pray in the name of Jesus that You would grant me a deeper and more meaningful dream life. I know that You are the God of dreams and visions and that You have a purpose and plan for my life that extends beyond my waking hours.

I ask that Your Holy Spirit would fill me and open my mind and heart to receive the messages and revelation You want to reveal to me through my dreams. Help me discern Your voice and will as I explore with You the deeper meanings and interpretations of the dreams You give me.

Lord, You have promised in John 16:13 to guide me in all truth and to teach me all things through Your Spirit. Guide me in my dream life and reveal to me the insights and wisdom I need in order to grow in my spiritual walk and fulfill Your calling on my life.

Protect me from any negative or harmful influences in my dreams and reveal to me Your truth and Your way. I trust in Your love and care for me, and I know that You have good plans for my life, plans to prosper me and not to harm me, plans to give me hope and a future, according to Jeremiah 29:11.

Thank You for the gift of dreams, for activating my dream life, and for the way that You use my dreams to bring me into a closer relationship with You. Give me the wisdom to steward the revelation You give me with obedience. And may my dreams be tools for Your glory and the good of those around me.

In Jesus's name I pray, amen.

A PRAYER TO REMEMBER DREAMS

Lord, I ask You to bless me with meaningful and significant dreams. And when I wake, help me to remember what You have shown me in my sleep, so that I may gain greater insight into Your will for my life. Holy Spirit, as the Teacher of all truth, bring to remembrance my dreams in Your timing and give me the grace to retain what You have shown me.

Lord, in Joel 2:28, You promise to pour out Your Spirit on all people, that we will see visions and dream dreams. I pray that You would open my spirit to experience more of You in my dreams, so that I may be empowered to live out Your purposes in my waking life.

I ask for protection from any negative or harmful dreams or influences and wisdom to discern Your voice and Your direction. Instruct me in the way of dream interpretation as You instructed Your prophet Jeremiah, in accordance with Your will and for Your glory.

In the name of Jesus, I pray. Amen.

A PRAYER FOR REVELATION

Jesus,

I thank You for making Yourself known to me, for pursuing me, and for loving me so well. You are the greatest desire of my heart—all I want is more of You. I know You long to reveal Yourself to Your children. Your Word says in 2 Chronicles 16:9 that Your eyes search the earth so that You may strengthen those whose hearts are fully committed to You. Here I am, Lord!

I ask You to pour out Your Spirit of wisdom and revelation upon me so that I may know You better and discern Your voice in my waking and sleeping hours. Help me to understand my dreams and to see them, myself, and the world around me the way You do.

You are the source of all wisdom and truth—lead me. As I read Your Word and spend time with You, open my spirit to Your truth alone, and give me a greater understanding of Your ways. Reveal to me the symbolism with which You are speaking in my dreams and give me the grace to understand any instructions, warnings, or assignments.

Show me how to pray into the visions and dreams You give, how to intercede based on what You show me. I commit to stewarding this gift with a heart of obedience.

Fill me with Your Holy Spirit, that I may be empowered to live a life that brings glory to Your name. May Your Spirit guide me into all truth and reveal to me the revelation that I need in order to know You more. Thank You for Your grace, mercy, and love, and for the hope that I have in You.

In Jesus's name, amen.

A PRAYER AGAINST NIGHTMARES

Heavenly Father,

As a child of God, I boldly declare Your protection and covering over my mind and spirit tonight as I sleep.

Guard me against any harmful or negative influences and protect me from nightmares and disturbing dreams. If there is any impure desire hidden in my heart, reveal it to me, Lord, so that I may surrender it to You.

If I have opened any doors that give the enemy access to my waking or sleeping life, reveal them to me and show me how to close those doors now. With the authority given to me by the power of Your Holy Spirit, I rebuke every attack against my sleep and I command the enemy to leave me now, in the name of Jesus.

I come into agreement with the angels on assignment in my life and release them to guard my bed, my home, and my property, and to divert any demonic attempts to torment me in my sleep.

I declare Your Word in Psalm 91:2 over myself tonight—that You are my refuge and my fortress, my God in whom I trust. I trust in Your loving care and Your watchful eye over me, and I ask that You would cover me and keep me safe from all harm.

Lord, Your perfect love casts out fear, so I give You my fears and my worries; replace them with Your perfect peace and Your comfort. Wrap me in Your presence so that I may rest in You.

Thank You for Your constant presence and Your unwavering love. I trust in Your power to protect me from all harm, both in waking life and in my dreams.

In Jesus's name I pray, amen.

APPENDIX A: DICTIONARY OF TERMS

This dictionary of terms serves as a comprehensive dream and symbolism reference guide. The dictionary contains the following:

- Male and female given names, providing spiritual and symbolic insights for deeper personal or dream interpretation.
- Various hues and colors that can be associated with references in Scripture, offering possible symbolism. As with every symbol, there may be various interpretations and meanings related to these colors based on the context within a dream.
- Biblical animals and objects that explore scriptural references to creatures and items, explaining their potential spiritual significance, meanings, and context within a dream.
- Locations, cities, and places, adding cultural and geographic context by detailing the origins and meanings of place names.

Combined, these terms create a cohesive tool for understanding and interpreting symbolic dream language.

A

AARON—"mountain of strength." The name Aaron can be interpreted as a spiritual reference to the strength and stability of God, which is often symbolized by mountains.

ABIGAIL—"father's joy." The name Abigail can be seen as a spiritual reference to the joy and love that come from a relationship with God.

ADA—"noble, happy." The name Ada can be interpreted as a spiritual reference to the idea of spiritual nobility and happiness.

ADAM—"man of the earth." The name Adam is associated with the biblical story of creation and can be interpreted as a spiritual reminder of humanity's origin and connection to the earth.

ADELAIDE—"noble kind."

AIDAN—"fiery one." The name Aidan is associated with fire, passion, and inspiration.

ALABAMA— named after the Alabama River, which was named after the Alabama people, a Native American tribe whose name means "thicket clearers."

ALAN—"rock, handsome." The name Alan can be interpreted as a reference to the steadfastness of God, often symbolized by rock and stone.

ALASKA—derived from the Aleut word "Alyeska," meaning "great land."

ALEXANDER/ALEX—"defender of the people." The name Alex can be interpreted as a spiritual reference to the idea of defending and protecting the weak and vulnerable.

ALEXANDRA—"defender of the people." The name Alexandra can be seen as a reference to the idea of being a protector and defender of others, humanity.

ALEXANDRIA—"defender of mankind."

ALICE—"noble." The name Alice can be interpreted as a spiritual reference to the idea of spiritual nobility and grace.

ALMOND—ta symbol of watchfulness and the idea of spiritual awakening and vigilance. (See Numbers 17:8; Jeremiah 1:11–12.)

ALMOND BRANCH—a symbol of God's faithfulness and the idea of spiritual renewal and new beginnings. (See Genesis 43:11; Exodus 25:33–34.)

ALTAR—a symbol of sacrifice and worship, the altar is associated with the idea of giving oneself fully to God. (See Genesis 12:7; Exodus 27:1–8; Hebrews 13:10.)

AMBER—glory of God, judgment, cleansing, fire. (See Ezekiel 1:4–27; Revelation 21:11.)

AMELIA—"industrious, striving." The name Amelia can be seen as a reference to the importance of spiritual striving and hard work.

AMETHYST—a purple gemstone that was one of the stones in the breastplate of the High Priest Aaron and cited as one of the stones in the foundations of the New Jerusalem, which represents God's perfect kingdom; the deep purple color of amethyst is associated with nobility and royalty; the Hebrew name for amethyst, *ahlamah,* literally means "dream stone." It was believed to induce pleasant dreams. (See Exodus 28:19; Revelation 21:20.)

AMETHYST—royalty, righteousness, devotion, luxury. (See Revelation 21:19–20.)

AMSTERDAM—"dam on the Amstel River."

ANDREW—"manly, warrior." The name Andrew can be seen as a spiritual reference to courage, strength, and determination in the face of adversity.

ANGEL—messengers of God often associated with the ideas of protection, guidance, and divine intervention. (See Matthew 18:10; Hebrews 1:14.)

ANNA—"grace." The name Anna can be interpreted as a spiritual reference to the idea of grace.

ANOINTING OIL—used in biblical times to consecrate people and objects; associated with the idea of setting something apart for God's purposes. (See Exodus 30:22–33; James 5:14.)

ANT—known for their hard work and diligence, ants are often used as an example of these qualities in the Bible. (See Proverbs 6:6–8.)

ANTHONY—"priceless one." The name Anthony can be interpreted as a spiritual reference to the value and worth of each individual soul.

AQUA—reference "sea." Baptism, Holy Spirit, healing, cleansing. (See Exodus 15:4; Ezekiel 47:5; John 3:5, 7:38–39.)

ARIEL—"lion of God." The name Ariel can be seen as a spiritual reference to the power and strength of God.

ARIZONA—named after the Pima Indian word *arizonac*, which means "little spring."

ARK—symbolizes salvation and God's protection in the story of Noah; a refuge from destruction. (See Genesis 6:11–9:19.)

ARKANSAS—named after the Quapaw tribe, whose name means "downstream people."

ARTHUR—"bear." The name Arthur can be seen as a spiritual reference to the strength and power of nature, often symbolized by the bear.

ASS/DONKEY—a humble and useful animal that was often used as a mode of transportation in biblical times. Jesus rode a donkey into Jerusalem, and the animal is also associated with the story of Balaam. (See Genesis 22:3; Numbers 22:21–35; Matthew 21:1–11.)

ATLANTA—"strength or youthful energy."

AUDREY—"noble strength." The name Audrey can be interpreted as a reference to the idea of spiritual strength and resilience.

AUSTIN—"great one." The name Austin can be interpreted as a spiritual reference to the greatness and majesty of God, who is often referred to as the Almighty.

AUSTIN—"great, magnificent."

AVA—"life." The name Ava can be seen as a spiritual reference to the idea of life as a sacred and precious gift from God.

AZURE—God's glory, heaven, the Holy Spirit. (See Exodus 24:10; Ezekiel 1:25–28.)

B

BALTIMORE—"lord or house of Lord Baltimore."

BARCELONA—"the ancient Barcino, possibly from the Phoenician term *baraka*."

BARON—"nobleman" or "baronial." In reference to the nobility of spirit; the name can also be seen as a reminder of the importance of humility and service to others, as many barons historically held positions of authority and leadership in their communities.

BASKET—associated with the idea of provision and abundance. (See Genesis 40:16–17; Matthew 14:20.)

BEAR—known for its ferocity and strength, this animal is used as a symbol of God's wrath and judgment. (See 2 Kings 2:23–24.)

BEATRICE—"bringer of joy." The name Beatrice can be interpreted as a reference to the idea of bringing joy and happiness to others.

BEE—symbol of honey, which includes God's provision and sweetness; honeybees also represent community and industry, as shown in their work ethic and role in a hive, which reminds us of the importance of working together towards a common goal. (See Deuteronomy 32:13; Psalm 19:10.)

BEHEMOTH—a large and powerful creature that is often interpreted as a hippopotamus or an elephant and is used as a symbol of God's creative power. (See Job 40:15–24.)

BEIJING—"northern capital."

BELFAST—"mouth of the River Farset."

BELGRADE—"white city."

BENJAMIN—"son of the right hand." The name Benjamin can be seen as a spiritual reference to the favor and blessing of God, often symbolized by the right hand in many spiritual traditions.

BERLIN—"swamp."

BETHANY—"house of figs." The name Bethany can be seen as a reference to the idea of the spiritual household and the importance of nurturing spiritual fruit.

BIRMINGHAM—"homestead of the people of the leader Beorma."

BLACK—sin, death, mourning, famine, judgment. (See Jeremiah 4:28; Lamentations 4:8; Revelation 6:5–6.)

BLUE—God's law, heaven, holiness, divine grace. (See Exodus 24:10; Numbers 15:38–39; 2 Chronicles 2:7; Ezekiel 1:26, 10:1.)

BLUSH—innocence, purity, chastity. (See Song of Solomon 5:10.)

BOSTON—"town or village with a church."

BRANDON—"beacon hill." The name Brandon is not typically associated with spiritual meanings.

BRASS—often associated with the idea of judgment and the fiery wrath of God. (See Isaiah 48:4; Daniel 10:6.)

BREAD—a symbol of sustenance and nourishment, as well as the Word of God. (See Matthew 6:11; John 6:35.)

BRIAN—"noble, strong." The name Brian can be seen as a spiritual reference to the qualities of nobility and strength, which are important spiritual traits.

BRISBANE—"a corruption of the name of the river after which the city is named."

BRONZE—a metal used in biblical times for weapons and tools, especially prior to the Iron Age, and associated with the idea of strength and endurance. (See Isaiah 60:17.)

BRONZE—judgment, strength, endurance. (See Numbers 21:5–9; Ezekiel 1:7; Revelation 2:18–29.)

BRONZE SERPENT—a symbol of healing and salvation, associated with the idea of looking to God for redemption. (See Numbers 21:4–9; John 3:14–15.)

BROOKLYN—"broken land."

BROWN—earthly things, humility, poverty. (See Genesis 30:32–43; 2 Samuel 19:35; Isaiah 50:6.)

BRUSSELS—"settlement in the marsh."

BUDAPEST—"water plus father; an allusion to the city's location near the Danube River."

BUENOS AIRES—"fair winds" or "good airs."

C

CAIRO—"the victorious city."

CALEB—"faithful, devoted." The name Caleb can be interpreted as a spiritual reference to the importance of faithfulness and devotion in spiritual practice.

CALGARY—"clear running water."

CALIFORNIA—named after a fictional island paradise from a Spanish novel, which was thought to be located somewhere in the New World.

CAMEL—a desert animal that was often used for transportation in biblical times; it is also used as a symbol of wealth and prosperity. (See Genesis 12:16, 24:10–64; Isaiah 60:6; Matthew 19:24.)

CAMERON—"crooked nose." The name Cameron is not typically associated with spiritual meanings.

CANDICE—"pure" or "glowing."

CAPE TOWN—"the meeting place."

CAROLINE—"free woman." The name Caroline can be interpreted as a spiritual reference to the idea of spiritual freedom and liberation.

CASABLANCA—"white house."

CHARLES—"free man." The name Charles can be interpreted as a spiritual reference to the concepts of freedom, liberation, and enlightenment.

CHARLOTTE—"free woman." The name Charlotte also means free woman, with the same spiritual connotations as Caroline.

CHASE—"to hunt." The name Chase is not typically associated with spiritual meanings.

CHICAGO—"wild onion."

CHLOE—"blooming." The name Chloe can be seen as a spiritual reference to the idea of spiritual growth and development.

CHRISTIAN—"follower of Christ." The name Christian is directly associated with the Christian faith and can be seen as a spiritual reference to the importance of following Christ's teachings and example.

CHRISTOPHER—"bearer of Christ." The name Christopher can be interpreted as a spiritual reference to the importance of carrying the message and teachings of Christ to others.

CLARA—"clear, bright." The name Clara can be interpreted as a reference to the idea of spiritual clarity.

CLAY JARS—a symbol of fragility and weakness, of us as human vessels, and also of the power of God at work in and through us. (See Judges 7:16–22; 2 Corinthians 4:7; John 2: 1–11.)

COLIN—"victorious people." The name Colin can be interpreted as a spiritual reference to the idea of triumph over adversity and the power of faith in achieving victory.

COLORADO—named after the Colorado River, which was named by the Spanish for its reddish color.

CONNECTICUT—named after the Connecticut River, which means "long tidal river" in the Algonquian language.

CONNOR—"lover of hounds." The name Connor is not typically associated with spiritual meanings.

COPENHAGEN—"merchant's harbor."

COPPER—a metal often associated with the idea of purity, refinement, and the testing of faith. (See Job 23:10; Malachi 3:3.)

COW—associated with the story of the golden calf, which the Israelites worshiped as an idol. (See Exodus 32:2–6.)

CRIMSON—sin, sacrifice, atonement, redemption. (See Isaiah 1:18; Nahum 2:3; Matthew 27:28; Revelation 19:13.)

CROSS—a symbol of Christ's sacrifice and redemption, as well as the means of salvation for believers. (See Galatians 6:14; Colossians 1:20.)

CROWN—a symbol of victory and reward, as well as the idea of spiritual authority and rulership. (See James 1:12; Revelation 4:4.)

CYAN—water, life, heaven. (See Ezekiel 1:22–26; Revelation 21:19.)

CYMBALS—associated with the idea of making a joyful noise; worship and praise. (See 2 Samuel 6:5; Psalm 150:5.)

D

DAISY—"day's eye." The name Daisy can be seen as a reference to the sun.

DALLAS—"meadow dwelling."

DAMASCUS—"well-watered land."

DANIEL—"God is my judge." The name Daniel is associated with the biblical figure of Daniel, who is known for his wisdom and faithfulness to God.

DAVID—"beloved." The name David is associated with the biblical figure of King David, who is known for his love of God and his many psalms.

DEBORAH/DEBRA—"bee." Deborah was a prophetess and judge who played a significant role in leading the Israelites to victory against their enemies, the Canaanites. Her story is told in the book of Judges, and she is often regarded as a symbol of courage, strength, and wisdom.

DEER—a symbol of agility and speed, this animal is often associated with God's grace and protection. (See Habakkuk 3:19.)

DELAWARE—named after Lord De La Warr, an early colonial governor of Virginia.

DELHI—"threshold."

DENVER—"green valley."

DETROIT—"strait."

DIAMOND—symbolic of valuable, covenant, strength/hardness/stubbornness, and the glory of God. (See Exodus 28:18; Ezekiel 28:13; Psalm 19:10–14.)

DIANA—"divine." The name Diana can be interpreted as a spiritual reference to the idea of the divine and the sacred.

DOG—considered an unclean animal in biblical times and often associated with lowly and unworthy things; however, common modern-day symbolism for dog is "friend" as in "man's best friend." (See Exodus 11:7.)

DOLPHIN (PORPOISE)—also called "porpoise skins"; their hides were used as ancient leather coverings for the tabernacle and with sandals; a symbol of covering; similar to whales, dolphins exhibit high intelligence and cognitive abilities and could possibly symbolize spiritual attunement; based on the species' apparent playfulness and affinity toward humans they could also symbolize friendship and fun. (See Exodus 26:14.)

DOMINIC—"of the Lord." The name Dominic can be seen as a spiritual reference to the importance of surrendering one's will to the will of God.

DOVE—a symbol of peace and the Holy Spirit, this animal is associated with Jesus's anointing by God after His baptism by John the Baptist. (See Genesis 8:8–12; Matthew 3:16.)

DRAGON—used as a symbol of Satan and his power. (See Isaiah 27:1.)

DUBLIN—"black pool."

DURBAN—"bay, port."

DYLAN—"son of the sea." The name Dylan is not typically associated with spiritual meanings.

E

EAGLE—a symbol of strength and freedom, this animal is often used to represent God's power and protection; it can also represent renewal of strength or vitality; also keen spiritual or prophetic vision/sight. (See Deuteronomy 32:11–12; Isaiah 40:31; Psalm 103:5.)

EDEN—"delight." The name Eden can be seen as a spiritual reference to the garden of Eden and the origin of creation and humanity.

EDINBURGH—"fortress of Edwin."

EDWARD—"wealthy guardian." The name Edward can be interpreted as a spiritual reference to the idea of God as a protective and nurturing guardian.

ELEANOR—"bright, shining one." The name Eleanor can be interpreted as a spiritual reference to the idea of shining one's spiritual light in the world.

ELEPHANT—(See **Behemoth**.)

ELIJAH—"my God is Yahweh." The name Elijah is associated with the biblical prophet Elijah, who is known for his devotion to God and his many miracles.

ELIZABETH—"God is my oath." The name Elizabeth can be seen as a spiritual reference to the importance of making a covenant with God.

ELLIOT—"Jehovah is God." The name Elliot can be seen as a spiritual reference to the importance of acknowledging the divine nature of God.

EMERALD—green gemstones often associated with authority and the presence of God. (See Exodus 28:18; Ezekiel 1:26; Revelation 4:3.)

EMERALD—growth, harmony, balance, immortality. (See Exodus 28:18; Ezekiel 1:28; Revelation 4:3.)

EMILY—"rival." The name Emily can be interpreted as a reference to the idea of competition and striving for excellence.

EMMA—"universal." The name Emma can be seen as a spiritual reference to the idea of the scope of God's presence, love, and compassion.

ERIC—"ruler, king." The name Eric can be interpreted as a spiritual reference to the idea of God as the ultimate ruler and king.

ESTHER—"star." The name Esther can be interpreted as a spiritual reference to the idea of the stars as symbols of God's power and majesty; also reference to the biblical character Esther, who saved Israel from genocide.

ETHAN—"strong, firm." The name Ethan can be seen as a spiritual reference to the importance of strength and resilience in the face of spiritual challenges.

EVAN—"God is gracious." The name Evan can be interpreted as a spiritual reference to the idea of grace, which is a central theme in many spiritual traditions.

F

FAITH—"faith, trust." The name Faith is rooted in biblical and theological concepts of reliance on God, steadfastness, and conviction.

FELICITY—"happiness, good fortune." The name Felicity can be seen as a spiritual reference to the idea of spiritual joy and contentment.

FIG—a symbol of fruitfulness and abundance, as well as the judgment of God. (See Matthew 21:18–20; Jeremiah 24:2–8.)

FIG TREE—often used as a symbol of fruitfulness and prosperity, it can also represent barrenness and judgment. (See Jeremiah 8:13; Matthew 21:18–22.)

FIRE—often symbolizes God's power, the Holy Spirit, purification, refinement, or judgment. (See Exodus 3:2; 1 Kings 18:38–39; Acts 2:3; 1 Peter 1:7.)

FISH—a common symbol of humanity in the New Testament, often used in stories and parables by Jesus. The fish is a symbol of Christ's followers; also sustenance, abundance, and provision. (See Matthew 4:19; John 21:6–11.)

FISHERMAN—a symbol of evangelism and the idea of spreading the gospel to others. (See Matthew 4:19; Mark 1:17.)

FLORENCE—"flourishing, prosperous." The name Florence can be interpreted as a spiritual reference to the idea of spiritual flourishing and abundance; also a city.

FLORIDA—named for the Spanish phrase *Pascua Florida,* meaning "flowery feast" or "feast of flowers."

FLUTE/PIPE—often used in celebrations and processions and associated with joy and merriment. (See Genesis 4:21; Daniel 3:5.)

FOX—often used as a symbol of cunning, deceit, and destruction. (See Judges 15:4; Song of Songs 2:25; Luke 13:32.)

FRANKFURT—"ford of the Franks."

FRANKINCENSE—associated with worship and purification. (See Exodus 30:34–38; Matthew 2:11.)

FUCHSIA—righteousness, holiness, royalty. (See Psalm 45:13–14; Isaiah 11:1–10.)

G

GABRIEL—"God is my strength." The name Gabriel is associated with the archangel Gabriel, who is known for his many messages from God.

GABRIELLA—"God is my strength." The name Gabriella can be seen as a spiritual reference to the importance of relying on God for strength and support.

GATES—often used as symbols of access and authority; associated with the idea of entering into God's presence. (See Genesis 22:17; Psalm 24:7–10.)

GAVIN—"white hawk." The name Gavin is not typically associated with spiritual meanings.

GENEVA—"juniper tree."

GENEVIEVE—"woman of the people." The name Genevieve can be interpreted as a spiritual reference to the idea of spiritual community and connection.

GEORGE—"farmer." The name George can be seen as a spiritual reference to the idea of cultivating one's spiritual garden and bearing spiritual fruit.

GEORGIA—named in honor of King George II of Great Britain.

GLASGOW—"green hollow."

GOAT—often used as a symbol of sin and atonement. (See Leviticus 16:7–26.)

GOLD—often used as a symbol of wealth, power, and purity. Can also be associated with royalty and the glory of God. (See Genesis 2:11–12; Matthew 2:11; 1 Kings 10:14; Psalm 19:10.) Divinity, glory, kingship, purity. (See Exodus 25:10–17; Psalm 21:3; Revelation 3:18.)

GRACE—"grace, favor." The name Grace is a direct reference to God's grace, a central theme in Christianity.

GRANT—"great, large." The name Grant can be interpreted as a spiritual reference to the greatness and majesty of God.

GRAPES—a symbol of abundance and joy, as well as the idea of spiritual fruitfulness. (See Numbers 13:23; John 15:5.)

GRAY—humility, mourning, repentance. (See Isaiah 1:18; Daniel 7:9; James 4:9.)

GREEN—growth, nature, health, prosperity. (See Psalm 23:2; Isaiah 40:8; Ezekiel 47:12; Revelation 8:7.) Some people also associate the color green with envy, jealousy, or covetousness. However, the Bible does not explicitly associate the color green with these negative emotions or attitudes.

H

HALIFAX—"holy hair."

HAMBURG—"castle on the hill."

HANNAH—"grace." The name Hannah can be seen as a spiritual reference to the idea of grace, which is a central theme in Christianity.

HARP—often used as a symbol of worship and praise; associated with the sounds of angels/heavenly realm. (See Genesis 4:21; Psalm 33:2; Revelation 14:2.)

HARPER—"harp player." The name Harper can be interpreted as a spiritual reference to music and praise.

HARRISON—"son of Harry." The name Harrison is not typically associated with spiritual meanings.

HAWAII—named after the largest island in the archipelago, which was named after Hawaii Loa, a legendary Polynesian navigator.

Hazel—"hazel tree." The name Hazel can be seen as a reference to trees or the color green.

HELSINKI—"Helsing's town."

HENRY—"ruler of the household." The name Henry can be seen as a spiritual reference to the idea of God as the ultimate ruler and head of the spiritual household.

HIPPOPOTAMUS—(See **Behemoth.**)

HONEY—often used as a symbol of sweetness and abundance, nourishment, the Word of God, and provision. (See Exodus 3:8; Ezekiel 3:3; Matthew 3:4.)

HONG KONG—"fragrant harbor."

HOPE—"hope." The name Hope is a direct reference to a central theme in Christianity, as in faith, hope, and love.

HORN—often used as a symbol of strength and power; associated with victory and triumph. It is also associated with the shofar, a horn that was used in Jewish worship and is still used today during the holidays of Rosh Hashanah and Yom Kippur. (See Joshua 6:4–20; Psalm 75:10.)

HORSE—often used as a symbol of power and strength, this animal is associated with war and conquest. (See Exodus 15:1–21; Revelation 6:1–8.)

HOUSTON—"hill town."

HYENA—associated with desolation and abandonment. (See Isaiah 34:14.)

I

IDAHO—the name Idaho is thought to be derived from a Shoshone phrase meaning "gem of the mountains."

ILLINOIS—named after the Illiniwek, a confederation of Native American tribes in the region.

IMOGEN—"innocent." The name Imogen can be interpreted as a spiritual reference to the idea of innocence and purity.

INCENSE—(1)a symbol of prayer and worship, as well as the idea of spiritual fragrance and a pleasing aroma. (See Psalm 141:2; Revelation 8:3–4.) (2)Used in biblical times as a symbol of prayer and worship; associated with the idea of offering oneself as a sacrifice to God. (See Exodus 30:34–38; Revelation 5:8.)

INDIANA—named after the Native American tribes that inhabited the area, possibly the Shawnee, whose name means "southerner."

INDIGO—royalty, authority, priesthood, grace. (See Exodus 25:4–7; Esther 8:15; Revelation 1:14, 5:5.)

IOWA—the name Iowa is derived from the Iowa River, which was named after the Iowa people, a Native American tribe whose name means "sleepy ones."

IRON—a metal often associated with strength, military might, and endurance, as well as the iron rule of God. (See Deuteronomy 8:9; Judges 4:3; Job 40:18.)

ISAAC—"he will laugh." The name Isaac is associated with the biblical figure of Isaac, who was born to Sarah and Abraham in their old age.

ISABELLA—"pledged to God." The name Isabella can be seen as a spiritual reference to the importance of making a covenant with God.

ISAIAH—"salvation of the Lord." The name Isaiah is associated with the biblical prophet Isaiah, who is known for his prophecies of redemption and salvation.

ISTANBUL—"to the city."

IVY—"ivy plant." The name Ivy can be interpreted as a spiritual reference to the idea of spiritual growth and development.

J

JACINTH—a purple gemstone often associated with the idea of royalty, majesty, and the glory of God. (See Revelation 9:17.)

JACK—"God is gracious." The name Jack can be interpreted as a spiritual reference to the idea of grace, which is a central theme in many spiritual traditions.

JACKSON—"son of Jack." The name Jackson is not typically associated with spiritual meanings.

JACOB—"supplanter." The name Jacob is associated with the biblical figure of Jacob, who wrestled with God and received the name Israel. (See Genesis 32:22–32.)

JADE—"jade stone." The name Jade can be seen as a reference to gemstones or the color green. Jade can also reference preciousness, perfection, and royalty. (See Exodus 28:20; Ezekiel 1:16; Revelation 21:11.)

JAKARTA—"victorious city."

JAMES—"supplanter." The name James can be seen as a spiritual reference to the importance of humility and surrender in spiritual growth.

JASMINE—"gift from God" or "fragrant flower." The name Jasmine can be interpreted as a spiritual reference to gifts from God; also a reference to beauty and pleasing aromas, as is symbolic of worship unto the Lord.

JASON—"healer." The name Jason can be interpreted as a spiritual reference to the power of healing, which is often associated with spiritual practices such as prayer and meditation.

JASPER—a gemstone often associated with authority, the glory of God, and the foundations of the New Jerusalem. It is also associated with the idea of stability and protection. (See Exodus 28:20; Revelation 21:11.)

JEREMIAH—"appointed by God." The name Jeremiah is associated with the biblical prophet Jeremiah, who is known for his prophecies of judgment and restoration.

JERUSALEM—"city of peace."

JESSE—"gift." The name Jesse can be interpreted as a spiritual reference to the idea of God's grace as a gift to humanity.

JESUS—"God saves." The name Jesus is directly associated with the Christian faith and can be seen as a spiritual reminder of the importance of salvation.

JOEL—"Jehovah is God." The name Joel can be seen as a spiritual reference to the importance of acknowledging the divine nature of God.

JOHANNESBURG—"John's town."

JOHN—"God is gracious." The name John is associated with the biblical figure of John the Baptist, who is known for his baptism of Jesus.

JONATHAN—"gift of God." The name Jonathan can be interpreted as a spiritual reference to gifts from God.

JORDAN—"to flow, descend." The name Jordan is associated with the Jordan River, which is a significant location in Israel.

JOSEPH—"he will add." The name Joseph is associated with the biblical figure of Joseph, to whom God spoke in many dreams; he was sold into slavery by his brothers but ultimately became a ruler in Egypt and helped preserve the family line of Israel.

JOSEPHINE—"God will add." The name Josephine can be seen as a spiritual reference to the idea of abundance and growth through God's blessings.

JOSHUA—"God is salvation." The name Joshua is associated with the biblical figure of Joshua, who led the Israelites into the promised land.

JOY—"joy." The name Joy is a direct reference to a central theme in Christianity.

JULIA—"youthful." The name Julia can be interpreted as a spiritual reference to the idea of youthfulness and vitality.

JULIET—"youthful." The name Juliet also means youthful, with the same spiritual connotations as Julia.

JUNE—"June, the sixth month of the year." The name June is associated with new beginnings, growth, and warmth.

JUSTIN—"just, righteous." The name Justin can be seen as a spiritual reference to the importance of justice and righteousness in spiritual practice.

K

KANSAS—named after the Kansa people, a Native American tribe whose name means "people of the south wind."

KARACHI—"the village of Kolachi."

KATHERINE—"pure." The name Katherine can be interpreted as a spiritual reference to the idea of purity and holiness.

KAYLA—"beloved." The name Kayla can be seen as a spiritual reference to the idea of God's love for humanity.

KENTUCKY—named after the Kentucky River, which was named after the Wyandot Indian word for "land of tomorrow."

KEVIN—"handsome, gentle." The name Kevin is not typically associated with spiritual meanings.

KIEV—"from the name of Kyi, one of the legendary founders of the city."

KUALA LUMPUR—"muddy confluence."

KYLE—"narrow, straight." The name Kyle can be interpreted as a spiritual reference to the importance of staying on the straight and narrow path in spiritual practice.

L

LAMB—a symbol of sacrifice and redemption, this animal is often associated with Jesus as the "Lamb of God," as well as with meekness and gentleness. (See Exodus 12:3–14; John 1:29.)

LAMP—a symbol of the Word of God and the light of Christ, as well as the ideas of guidance and revelation. (See Psalm 119:105; John 1:9.)

LAS VEGAS—"the meadows."

LAVENDER—"spikenard" in Scripture; beauty, glory, sweetness, fragrance. (See Song of Solomon 4:13–14.)

LAVER/BASIN—also associated with tub, sink, or bathroom, this item was used for washing in biblical times and is associated with the idea of cleansing and purification. (See Exodus 30:17–21; John 13:8.)

LEAH—"weary." The name Leah can be interpreted as a spiritual reference to the idea of finding rest and peace in God.

LEAVEN/YEAST—often used as a symbol of the insidious nature of sin and corruption. (See Exodus 12:15–20; Matthew 13:33.)

LEOPARD—often used as a symbol of speed and agility. (See Jeremiah 5:6; Daniel 7:6.)

LEVIATHAN—a sea monster or dragon that is often used as a symbol of chaos and evil but is also associated with God's power and control over creation. (See Job 41:1–34; Psalm 104:25–26.)

LIAM—"strong-willed warrior." The name Liam can be seen as a spiritual reference to the strength and resilience required for spiritual growth and development.

LILAC—renewal, peace, beauty, fragrance. (See Song of Solomon 2:1–2.)

LILY—often used as symbols of beauty and purity, this plant is associated with the idea of trusting in God's provision. It can also seen as a spiritual reference to the importance of beauty and purity in spiritual practice. (See Song of Solomon 2:1; Matthew 6:28–29.)

LILLIAN—"lily flower." The name Lillian also means lily flower, with the same spiritual connotations as Lily.

LIMA—"name of a plant that grows in the region."

LION—a symbol of strength and courage, this animal is often used to represent God's power and protection; lions are natural predators, and so any predatory attributes can symbolize sin, as in *"crouching at the door"* (Genesis 4:7). (See Judges 14:5–9; Daniel 6:1–28; Genesis 4:7.)

LIONESS—often used as a symbol of strength and courage, this animal is associated with the fierceness of motherhood. (See Proverbs 30:30.)

LISBON—"safe harbor."

LIV—"life." The name Livia can be seen as a spiritual reference to the idea of life as a sacred and precious gift from God.

LIZARD—considered unclean animals in biblical times. (See Leviticus 11:30.)

LOCUST—often used as a symbol of destruction and judgment. (See Exodus 10:1–20; Matthew 3:4.)

LOGAN—"small hollow." The name Logan is not typically associated with spiritual meanings.

LOLA—"sorrows." The name Lola can be interpreted as a spiritual reference to the idea of finding comfort and solace in God.

LONDON—"fortress of the moon."

LORELEI—"alluring enchantress." The name Lorelei can be seen as a reference to the idea of spiritual wonder.

LOS ANGELES—"the angels."

LOUISE—"renowned warrior." The name Louise can be interpreted as a spiritual reference to the idea of being a spiritual warrior and champion.

LOUISIANA—named in honor of King Louis XIV of France.

LUCAS—"bringer of light." The name Lucas can be interpreted as a spiritual reference to the idea of bringing light and illumination to the world.

LUCY—"light." The name Lucy can be seen as a spiritual reference to the light of Christ in us, the Light of the world.

LUKE—"bringer of light." The name Luke also means bringer of light, with the same spiritual connotations as Lucas.

LYDIA—"from Lydia." The name Lydia can be interpreted as a spiritual reference to Lydia from the book of Acts; Lydia was a wealthy businesswoman who, along with her entire family, was baptized by Paul, and considered the first documented Christian convert in Europe.

M

MADELINE—"high tower." The name Madeline can be seen as a spiritual reference to the idea of spiritual strength and fortification.

MADRID—"place of many streams."

MAINE—named after the French province of Maine.

MANCHESTER—"fortress of the men of Mamucium."

MANILA—"white flower."

MARGARET—"pearl." The name Margaret can be interpreted as a spiritual reference to the idea of spiritual treasure, as in the pearl of great price.

MARIA—"bitter, or beloved." The name Maria can be seen as a spiritual reference to the importance of both bitterness and sweetness in spiritual growth; also associated with the New Testament figures of Mary, the mother of Jesus, and Mary Magdelene.

MAROON—sacrifice, sin, passion. (See Leviticus 14:52; Isaiah 1:18; Matthew 27:28–29.)

MARY—"bitter, or beloved." The name Mary can be interpreted as a spiritual reference to the importance of both bitterness and sweetness in spiritual growth; also associated with the New Testament figures of Mary, the mother of Jesus, and Mary Magdelene.

MARYLAND—named in honor of Queen Henrietta Maria, the wife of King Charles I of England.

MASON—"worker in stone." The name Mason can be interpreted as a spiritual reference to the idea of building the spiritual temple and laying a strong foundation for spiritual practice.

MASSACHUSETTS—named after the Massachusett tribe, whose name means "at the large hill."

MATILDA—"mighty in battle." The name Matilda can be seen as a spiritual reference to the idea of spiritual warfare and the importance of being a spiritual warrior.

MATTHEW—"gift of God." The name Matthew is associated with the biblical figure of Matthew, who was a tax collector before becoming one of Jesus's disciples.

MAUVE—strength, courage, distinguished. (See Song of Solomon 5:10.)

MAX—"greatest." The name Max can be seen as a spiritual reference to the greatness and majesty of God.

MAYA—"illusion." The name Maya can be interpreted as a spiritual reference to the idea of spiritual deception or counterfeits, and the importance of seeing beyond appearances.

MELBOURNE—"mill stream."

MIA—"mine, bitter." The name Mia can be seen as a spiritual reference to the importance of claiming ownership over one's spiritual life.

MIAMI—"sweet water."

MICHAEL—"Who is like God?" The name Michael is associated with the archangel Michael, who is known for his protection and guidance of humanity.

MICHIGAN—the name Michigan is thought to be derived from the Ojibwe Indian word *mishigamaa,* meaning "large water" or "large lake."

MILAN—"gracious, dear."

MILK—a symbol of spiritual nourishment and the idea of spiritual growth and maturity. (See1 Peter 2:2; Hebrews 5:12–14.)

MINNEAPOLIS—"city of waters."

MINNESOTA—the name Minnesota is thought to be derived from the Dakota Indian word *minisota,* meaning "cloudy water."

MIRRORS—associated with the idea of seeing ourselves as God sees us and of reflecting the image of Christ. (See Exodus 38:8; 1 Corinthians 13:12.)

MISSISSIPPI—named after the Mississippi River, which means "great river" in the Ojibwe language.

MISSOURI—named after the Missouri River, which means "town of the large canoes" in the Native American language of the Illinois people.

MOLE—considered an unclean animal in biblical times. (See Leviticus 11:29.)

MONTANA—the name Montana is derived from the Spanish word *montaña,* meaning "mountain."

MONTREAL—"Mount Royal."

MOSCOW—"by the Moscow River."

MUMBAI—"mother goddess."

MUNICH—"by the monks."

MUSTARD SEED—a symbol of faith and the idea of spiritual growth. (See Matthew 13:31–32; Luke 17:6.)

MYRRH—a type of spice used in ancient times for embalming and perfume; associated with the idea of suffering and sacrifice. (See Genesis 37:25; Matthew 2:11.)

N

NAOMI—"pleasantness." The name Naomi can be interpreted as a reference to the idea of spiritual beauty and pleasantness; also a reference to the biblical character of Naomi, mother-in-law of Ruth.

NAPLES—"new city."

NASHVILLE—"town of the hills."

NATALIE—"birthday of the Lord." The name Natalie can be seen as a spiritual reference to the importance of celebrating the birth of Christ.

NATASHA—"born on Christmas Day." The name Natasha also refers to Christmas, with the same spiritual connotations as Natalie.

NATHAN—"gift from God." The name Nathan can be interpreted as a spiritual reference to the idea of all of life as a gift from God.

NATHANIEL—"gift of God." The name Nathaniel also means gift of God, with the same spiritual connotations as Nathan.

NEBRASKA—the name Nebraska is thought to be derived from a Native American word meaning "flat water."

NET—associated with the idea of evangelism and spreading the gospel, and with accomplishing the will of God. (See Matthew 4:19; Mark 1:17.)

NEVADA—named after the Sierra Nevada mountains, which means "snowy range" in Spanish.

NEW HAMPSHIRE—named after the English county of Hampshire, which means "village-town."

NEW JERSEY—named after the English Channel Island of Jersey.

NEW MEXICO—named after the country of Mexico, which was named after the Aztec city of Mexica-Tenochtitlan.

NEW ORLEANS—"named after Philippe II, Duke of Orleans."

NEW YORK—"New Amsterdam." Originally a Dutch settlement. Renamed New York after the English took over New Amsterdam in honor of the Duke of York (later King James II of England).

NICHOLAS—"victory of the people." The name Nicholas can be seen as a spiritual reference to the idea of victory over sin and adversity.

NICOLE—"victory of the people." The name Nicole can be seen as a spiritual reference to the idea of spiritual victory and triumph.

NOAH—"rest, comfort." The name Noah is associated with the biblical figure of Noah, who obeyed God's instructions to build an ark to save himself and his family from the great flood.

NOELLE—"Christmas." The name Noelle can be interpreted as a spiritual reference to the importance of celebrating the birth of Christ.

NOLAN—"champion." The name Nolan can be seen as a spiritual reference to the importance of perseverance and determination in spiritual practice.

NORA—"honor." The name Nora can be seen as a spiritual reference to the idea of spiritual honor and integrity.

NORTH CAROLINA—named in honor of King Charles I of England, whose Latin name is Carolus.

NORTH DAKOTA—the name Dakota is derived from the Dakota Sioux Indian word for "friend."

O

OHIO—named after the Ohio River, which means "great river" in the Iroquois language.

OIL—used for anointing and healing in biblical times; associated with the idea of being set apart for God's purposes. (See Exodus 30:22–33; James 5:14.)

OKLAHOMA—derived from the Choctaw Indian words *okla* and *humma,* which together mean "red people."

OLIVE BRANCH—a symbol of peace and the idea of spiritual renewal and restoration; olive trees are evergreen, further symbolizing bearing fruit in all seasons. (See Genesis 8:11; Psalm 52:8; Romans 11:17–24.)

OLIVE OIL—a symbol of anointing and consecration, as well as of the Holy Spirit and the healing of the body and soul. (See Exodus 29:7; James 5:14.)

OLIVE—peace, abundance, divine fruitfulness, eternal life. (See Genesis 8:11; Zechariah 4:3; John 15:1–10; Romans 11:16–24.)

OLIVER—"olive tree." The name Oliver can be interpreted as a spiritual reference to oil, which has numerous symbolic meanings and is referenced frequently in Scripture; as it is an evergreen tree, it can also be interpreted to represent the tree of life as referenced in the book of Ezekiel.

OLIVIA—"olive tree." The name Olivia can be interpreted as a spiritual reference to oil, which has numerous symbolic meanings and is referenced frequently in Scripture; as it is an evergreen tree, it can also be interpreted to represent the tree of life as referenced in the book of Ezekiel.

ORANGE—fire, judgment, the fall, hope. (See Ezekiel 1:4; Joel 2:3; Revelation 6:12, 20:15.)

OREGON—named after the Columbia River, which was originally named the "River of the West" by American explorers.

OSLO—"the mouth of the Lo river."

OSTRICH—often used as a symbol of foolishness and neglect, as it is described as abandoning its eggs. (See Job 39:13–18; Lamentations 4:3.)

OTTAWA—"to trade."

OWEN—"youthful warrior." The name Owen can be seen as a spiritual reference to the idea of spiritual warfare and the importance of being a spiritual warrior.

OX—a symbol of strength and service, this animal is often used to represent Jesus as a servant. (See Deuteronomy 25:4; Luke 14:5.)

P

PAIGE—"servant, helper." The name Paige can be seen as a spiritual reference to the importance of service and humility in spiritual growth.

PAPYRUS (PAPER)—used in biblical times for writing and making paper; associated with recording and preserving God's Word. (See Exodus 2:3; Isaiah 18:2.)

PARIS—"city of light."

PATRICK—"nobleman." The name Patrick is associated with Saint Patrick, the patron saint of Ireland, who is known for spreading Christianity throughout the country.

PAUL—"small." The name Paul can be seen as a spiritual reference to the importance of humility in spiritual growth and development.

PEACOCK—is associated with wealth and abundance, this animal was often given as an exotic gift. (See 1 Kings 10:22.)

PEARL—often associated with the idea of great value and worth, as well as with purity and the kingdom of God. (See Matthew 13:45–46; Revelation 21:21.)

PENELOPE—"weaver." The name Penelope can be seen as a spiritual reference to the importance of weaving together the different strands of life.

PENNSYLVANIA—named in honor of William Penn, the father of the founder of the Pennsylvania Colony.

PERFUME—used in biblical times as a symbol of beauty and luxury; associated with the ideas of worship and devotion. (See Song of Solomon 1:3; Mark 14:3–9.)

PERTH—"meeting place."

PETER—"rock." The name Peter is associated with the biblical figure of Peter, who is known for his faithfulness to Jesus and his leadership of the early Christian church.

PHILADELPHIA—"brotherly love."

PHILIP—"lover of horses." The name Philip can be interpreted as a spiritual reference to the idea of spiritual travel, which is often symbolized by horses in many spiritual traditions.

PHOEBE—"bright, shining." The name Phoebe can be interpreted as a spiritual reference to the idea of shining the light of Christ in the world.

PHOENIX—"mythical bird that is reborn from the ashes of its predecessor."

PIGEON—often used as a sacrifice in biblical times. (See Leviticus 1:14–17.)

PINK—love, joy, comfort, gentleness. (See Isaiah 40:11; Song of Solomon 5:16; Philippians 1:9–10.)

PIPER—"pipe player." The name Piper may be seen as a reference to the importance of music and sound in worship.

PITTSBURGH—"fortress of Pitt."

POMEGRANATE—a symbol of abundance and fertility, as well as the idea of spiritual fruitfulness. (See Numbers 13:23; Song of Solomon 4:3.)

PORTLAND—"land surrounding a harbor."

PRAGUE—"threshold or doorstep."

PROVIDENCE—"divine guidance or protection."

PURPLE—royalty, wealth, divinity, authority. (See Judges 8:26; Esther 8:15–17; Mark 15:17–18; Revelation 17:4.)

Q

QUAIL—a source of food/provision for the Israelites during their desert journey; the Israelites' craving for these birds was also a source of God's judgment. (See Exodus 16:1–36; Numbers 11:4–35.)

QUEBEC CITY—"where the river narrows."

QUINN—"wise." The female name Quinn can be interpreted as a spiritual reference to the importance of wisdom. The male name Quinn can be seen as a spiritual reference to the importance of wisdom in spiritual growth and development.

R

RACHEL—"ewe." The name Rachel can be seen as a spiritual reference to the importance of caring for and nurturing others; also possible reference to the biblical character Rachel, who was the wife of Jacob and mother of Joseph and Benjamin.

RAINBOW—a symbol of God's promise and the idea of spiritual renewal and restoration. (See Genesis 9:12–16; Revelation 4:3.)

RAM—often used as a sacrifice in biblical times, this animal is associated with obedience and submission. (See Genesis 22:13; Leviticus 16:3–34.)

RAVEN—found in the story of Noah, this bird was also sent by God to feed Elijah during a severe drought, symbolizing God's provision and care. (See Genesis 8:6–7; 1 Kings 17:4.)

RAYMOND—"wise protector." The name Raymond can be interpreted as a spiritual reference to the idea of God as a wise and protective guide.

REBECCA—"captivating." The name Rebecca can be interpreted as a spiritual reference to the importance of spiritual attraction and connection.

RED—blood, sacrifice, atonement, sin. (See Leviticus 14:52; Isaiah 1:18; Matthew 27:28–29; Revelation 6:4.)

REYKJAVIK—"bay of smoke."

RHODE ISLAND—named after the Greek island of Rhodes.

RICHARD—"brave ruler." The name Richard can be seen as a spiritual reference to the idea of God as the ultimate ruler and king.

RIO DE JANEIRO—"January River."

RIVER—a symbol of the Holy Spirit and the idea of spiritual life and growth. (See Ezekiel 47:1–12; John 7:37–39.)

ROBERT—"bright fame." The name Robert can be interpreted as a spiritual reference to the idea of shining one's spiritual light in the world.

ROME—"strength, force, courage."

ROPE—often used as a symbol of unity and strength; associated with the idea of God as a source of support and connection. (See Judges 16:11–12; Ecclesiastes 4:12.)

ROSE—(1) "rose flower." The name Rose can be seen as a spiritual reference to blooming, blossoming, and beauty. (2) love, beauty, Christ, sacrifice. (See Song of Solomon 2:1–2; John 3:16.)

RUBY—(1) "ruby gemstone." The female name Ruby can be interpreted as a spiritual reference to wisdom, virtue, and the value of a godly character; rubies appear in the Bible in the books of Exodus, Job, Proverbs, Isaiah, Ezekiel, and Lamentations. (2) Rubies are precious gemstones often associated with the idea of passion, love, and life. (See Proverbs 3:15–18.)

RUTH—"companion, friend." The name Ruth can be seen as a spiritual reference to the importance of spiritual companionship and friendship.

RYAN—"little king." The name Ryan can be seen as a spiritual reference to the idea of surrendering one's will to the divine will.

S

SABRINA—"patience." The name Sabrina can be interpreted as a spiritual reference to one of the fruit of the Spirit.

SACKCLOTH—a coarse fabric used in biblical times for mourning and repentance; associated with the ideas of humility and contrition. (See Genesis 37:34; Revelation 6:12.)

SALT—a symbol of preservation and purification, as well as of the idea of the covenant of God. (See Leviticus 2:13; Matthew 5:13.)

SAMANTHA—"listener." The name Samantha can be seen as a spiritual reference to the importance of listening and attuning to God's voice.

SAMUEL—"asked of God." The name Samuel is associated with the biblical figure of Samuel, who was a prophet and judge in Israel.

SAN DIEGO—"Saint James."

SAN FRANCISCO—"Saint Francis."

SAN JOSE—"Saint Joseph."

SAND—a symbol of God's promise, multiplication, and boundaries, as well as of instability. (See Genesis 22:17; Isaiah 10:22; Matthew 7:24–27.)

SANDALS (SHOES)—footwear associated with the idea of readiness and preparation to spread the gospel, as well as your Christian "walk." (See Exodus 3:5; Ephesians 6:15.)

SANTIAGO—"Saint James."

SAO PAULO—"Saint Paul."

SAPPHIRE—a blue gemstone often associated with the glory of God. (See Exodus 24:10; Job 28:16.)

SARAH—"princess." The name Sarah can be interpreted as a spiritual reference to royalty and nobility; also possible reference to the biblical figure Sarah, to whom God promised a son despite her old age.

SAVANNAH—"treeless plain." The name Savannah can be seen as a spiritual reference to the importance of open space and emptiness in spiritual practice.

SCARLET—sin, sacrifice, redemption, victory. (See Isaiah 1:18; Matthew 27:28–29; Revelation 12:11.)

SCARLETT—"red/scarlet." The name Scarlett can be interpreted as a reference to the color red; also possible reference to atoning blood/sacrifice of Jesus.

SCORPION—often used as a symbol of evil and judgment. (See Luke 10:19; Revelation 9:3–10.)

SEAN—"God is gracious." The name Sean is associated with the Irish form of John and can be interpreted as a spiritual reference to the idea of grace.

SEATTLE—"chief or elder."

SEBASTIAN—"venerable, revered." The name Sebastian can be seen as a spiritual reference to the idea of venerating and revering the divine.

SEOUL—"capital."

SERAPHINA—"fiery, burning." The name Seraphina can be seen as a spiritual reference to the idea of spiritual fire and passion.

SETH—"appointed." The name Seth is associated with the biblical figure of Seth, who was the third son of Adam and Eve.

SHANGHAI—"on the sea."

SHEEP—a symbol of guidance and protection, this animal is often used to represent God's care for His people. (See Psalm 23; John 10:1–18.)

SHEPHERD—a symbol of Christ and His care for His followers, as well as of the ideas of spiritual guidance and protection. (See Psalm 23:1; John 10:11–16.)

SHEPHERD'S STAFF—a possible symbol of guidance and protection. (See Genesis 32:10; Psalm 23:4.)

SHIELD—associated with the idea of God as a shield and protector. (See Psalm 3:3; Ephesians 6:16.)

SHIP—a symbol of the ideas of faith and trust in God, as well as of the journey of life. (See Acts 27:9–44; Hebrews 6:19.)

SILVER—(1) a precious metal often associated with the ideas of purity, redemption, refining of faith, and God's promises. (See Psalm 12:6; Zechariah 13:9.) (2) redemption, wisdom, purity, faith. (See Genesis 23:15–16; Psalm 12:6; Proverbs 2:4; Zechariah 13:9.)

SINGAPORE—"lion city."

SKY BLUE—heaven, divine revelation, the Holy Spirit. (See Exodus 24:10; Ezekiel 1:25–28; Matthew 3:16.)

SLATE—humility, mourning, repentance. (See Isaiah 57:15.)

SMOKE—a symbol of God's presence and the idea of spiritual purification and refinement. (See Exodus 19:18; Revelation 15:8.)

SNAKE/SERPENT—often used as a symbol of evil and deception, as seen in the story of Adam and Eve. However, in the New Testament, Jesus tells His disciples to be as wise as serpents. Additionally, in both Numbers 21:4–9 and John 3:14–15, the bronze serpent was a symbol of healing and salvation and is associated with the idea of looking to God for redemption. (See Genesis 3:1–24; Numbers 21:4–9; Matthew 10:16.)

SOFIA—"wisdom."

SOPHIA—"wisdom." The name Sophia can be interpreted as a direct reference to the importance of wisdom.

SOUTH CAROLINA—named in honor of King Charles I of England, whose Latin name is Carolus.

SOUTH DAKOTA—the name Dakota is derived from the Dakota Sioux Indian word for "friend."

SPARROW—often used as a symbol of God's care for even the smallest creatures, this animal is associated with the idea that God watches over and protects all living things. (See Psalm 84:3; Matthew 10:29–31.)

SPEAR—symbol of weapons or of God as a conqueror and warrior. (See Judges 5:8; Ephesians 6:17.)

SPIDER—often used as a symbol of vanity and futility; a spider's web can be a metaphor for a trap or snare for believers; also deceit as in "spinning a web of lies." (See Isaiah 59:5.)

STELLA—"star." The name Stella can be seen as a spiritual reference to the importance of the stars as symbols of God's power and majesty.

STEPHANIE—"crown." The name Stephanie can be interpreted as a spiritual reference to the ideas of spiritual royalty and authority.

STEPHEN—"crown." The name Stephen is associated with the biblical figure of Stephen, who was the first Christian martyr.

STOCKHOLM—"log island."

STONE/ROCK—often used as a symbol of strength and stability; can also be associated God as a firm foundation and Jesus as cornerstone. (See 1 Samuel 17:40; Matthew 16:18; Joshua 4:20–24; 1 Peter 2:4–8.)

STORK—listed as "unclean" in Leviticus; mentioned in the Psalms as one of the God's creatures (both large and small) receiving care and protection; modern symbolism can relate to motherhood or pregnancy. (See Leviticus 11:19; Psalm 104:17.)

SUSAN—"lily flower." The name Susan can be seen as a spiritual reference to the importance of beauty and purity.

SWALLOW—often used as a symbol of faithfulness and loyalty. (See Psalm 84:3; Jeremiah 8:7.)

SWORD—may symbolize divine retribution or the Word of God as a powerful weapon against evil. (See Genesis 3:24; Hebrews 4:1; Ephesians 6:17.)

SYDNEY—"wide meadow."

T

TAIPEI—"terrace pond."

TAMBOURINE—often associated with celebration, joy, and exuberance. (See Exodus 15:20; Psalm 150:4.)

TANNER—"leather worker." The name Tanner is not typically associated with spiritual meanings.

TAYLOR—"tailor." The name Taylor is not typically associated with spiritual meanings.

TEHRAN—"warm slope."

TEL AVIV—"hill of spring."

TEMPLE—a symbol of ourselves as the carriers of God's presence. (See 1 Corinthians 3:16–17; Revelation 21:22.)

TENNESSEE—named after the Cherokee village of Tanasi, which means "a great river" in the Cherokee language.

TENT—may symbolize pilgrimage and transition (non-permanent dwelling); also may represent our bodies as a temporary home for the Holy Spirit. (See Hebrews 11:9–10; 2 Corinthians 5:1–4.)

TESSA—"harvester." The name Tessa can be interpreted as a spiritual reference to the importance of spiritual harvest and abundance.

TEXAS—derived from the Caddo Indian word *tayshas*, meaning "friends" or "allies."

THALIA—"blossoming." The name Thalia can be seen as a spiritual reference to the idea of spiritual growth and development.

THEODORE—"gift of God." The name Theodore can be interpreted as a spiritual reference to the idea of all of life as a gift from God.

THOMAS—"twin." The name Thomas is associated with the biblical figure of Thomas, who doubted Jesus's resurrection until he saw Him with his own eyes.

THORNS—often used as symbols of pain and suffering; associated with the idea of Christ's sacrifice on the cross. (See Genesis 3:18; Matthew 27:29.)

TIGER—not mentioned in the Bible, these animals are not native to the Middle East; consider other "big cat" symbolism, such as power and ferocity; tigers are natural predators, and so any predatory attributes can symbolize sin, as in "crouching at the door." (See Job 4:10–11; Genesis 4:7.)

TIMOTHY—"honoring God." The name Timothy can be seen as a spiritual reference to the importance of honoring God in all aspects of life.

TIN—a metal often associated with the idea of purity and the refining of faith, as well as of the idea of weakness and imperfection. (See Ezekiel 22:18–20.)

TOKYO—"eastern capital."

TOMB/GRAVE—associated with the idea of generations, death, and resurrection. (See Genesis 23:1–20; Matthew 27:60; John 20:1–10.)

TOPAZ—a gemstone often associated with the idea of divine fire and enlightenment. (See Job 28:19.)

TORONTO—"meeting place."

TREE—may symbolize life, growth, strong faith, health; specific types of trees may have other, more specific meanings. (See Genesis 2:9; Psalm 1:3; Ezekiel 47:12; Galatians 5:22–23.)

TRUMPET—associated with the idea of announcement and God's voice calling out to His people. (See Exodus 19:16; Revelation 8:6.)

TYLER—"maker of tiles." The name Tyler is not typically associated with spiritual meanings.

U

UNICORN—a mythical creature that is used interchangeably with "wild ox" in the King James translation as a symbol of strength and power. (See Numbers 23:22; Deuteronomy 33:17; Job 39:9–10.)

UTAH—named after the Ute tribe, whose name means "people of the mountains."

V

VALERIE—"strength, health." The name Valerie can be interpreted as a spiritual reference to the idea of spiritual strength and well-being.

VANCOUVER—"someone who comes from Coevorden," a Dutch city from which the name was derived.

VANESSA—"butterfly." The name Vanessa can be seen as a spiritual reference to transformation.

VERMONT—named after the French phrase *les verts monts,* meaning "the green mountains."

VICTORIA—"victory." The name Victoria can be interpreted as a reference to the idea of spiritual victory and triumph.

VINCENT—"conquering." The name Vincent can be seen as a spiritual reference to the idea of overcoming sin and adversity.

VINE—a symbol of Christ, as well as of spiritual growth and the fruitfulness of faith. (See John 15:1–8; Romans 11:16–24.)

VINEYARD—a symbol of God's provision and the ideas of spiritual fruitfulness and abundance. (See Isaiah 5:1–7; John 15:1–8.)

VIOLET—"violet flower." The name Violet can be seen as a reference to royalty.

VIPER—often used as a symbol of danger and death; being bitten by a viper specifically can symbolize being personal harmed in some way. (See Isaiah 30:6; Acts 28:3.)

VIRGINIA—named in honor of Queen Elizabeth I of England, who was known as the "Virgin Queen."

W

WASHINGTON—named in honor of President George Washington.

WATER—often used as a symbol of life, creation, sustenance, renewal, the Holy Spirit, and the idea of spiritual cleansing and renewal; the color and type of water in a dream also may signal further meaning (dirty, clear, deep, fresh, salt/ocean). (See Genesis 1:2; Exodus 17:6; John 4:10–14, 7:37–39; Ephesians 5:26; Titus 3:5.)

WESLEY—"western meadow." The name Wesley can be interpreted as a spiritual reference to the idea of spiritual growth as a journey through life.

WEST VIRGINIA—named for the western counties of Virginia that refused to secede from the Union during the Civil War.

WHALE—only referenced biblically in the story of Jonah when he is famously swallowed, then spat up three days later; as whales are considered to be among the most intelligent animals on earth, demonstrating advanced communication and cognitive abilities, they can symbolize spiritual intelligence and attunement to the Holy Spirit. (See Jonah 1:17.)

WHEAT—a symbol of the bread of life, as well as of the idea of spiritual nourishment and growth. (See Matthew 13:31–32; John 6:35.)

WHITE—purity, holiness, righteousness, victory. (See Psalm 51:7; Isaiah 1:18; Revelation 3:5, 7:14.)

WILLIAM—"resolute protector." The name William can be seen as a spiritual reference to the idea of God as a protective and resolute guardian.

WIND—a symbol of the power of God and also of the Holy Spirit; the Bible does associate the "four winds" (north, south, east, and west) metaphorically bringing destruction (east hot, dry desert wind), deliverance (west), warmth, blessing, and provision (south), and soothing, calming coolness and rain (north); depending on the context, wind can bring correction and change. (See John 3:8; Acts 2:2–4; East Wind—Genesis 41:23, Exodus 10:13, Jeremiah 4:11–12; West Wind—Exodus 10:19; North Wind—Song of Solomon 4:16; South Wind—Song of Solomon 4:16.)

WINE—(1) often used as a symbol of joy and celebration; associated with the idea of the new covenant and Christ's blood shed for our redemption; warning. (See Genesis 9:20–21; Psalm 104:14–15; Proverbs 20:1; Matthew 26:27–29.) (2) color. Blood, sacrifice, joy, abundance. (See Genesis 49:11; Psalm 104:14–15; Matthew 26:27–29.)

WINEPRESS—a symbol of judgment, as well as the idea of spiritual discipline and the refining of faith. (See Isaiah 63:1–3; Revelation 14:19–20.)

WISCONSIN—the name Wisconsin is derived from the Ojibwe Indian word *wiskonsin*, meaning "place of the beaver."

WOLF—often used as a symbol of aggression and danger; in Isaiah, it is used to represent peace and harmony in the future kingdom of God; consider any predatory context related to Satan as "devourer." (See Genesis 49:27; Isaiah 11:6–9.)

WOOD—may symbolize fuel, building/construction, humanity, the cross of Christ. (See Genesis 6:14, 22:3; Matthew 16:24.)

WOOL—a symbol of purity and righteousness. (See Isaiah 1:18; Revelation 7:14.)

WORM—often used as a symbol of weakness, insignificance, or suffering. (See Job 25:6; Isaiah 14:11.)

WYATT—"brave in war." The name Wyatt can be seen as a spiritual reference to the idea of spiritual warfare and the importance of being a spiritual warrior.

WYOMING—named after the Wyoming Valley in Pennsylvania, which means "extensive meadows" in the Delaware Indian language.

X

XAVIER—"new house." The name Xavier can be interpreted as a spiritual reference to the idea of spiritual transformation and renewal.

Y

YAK—often used as a symbol of strength and power. (See Job 39:9–10.)

YELLOW—faith, glory, light, divine power. Please note that while some people may associate the color yellow with fear, the Bible does not explicitly make this connection. (See Ecclesiastes 11:7; Matthew 17:2; Revelation 1:12–16.)

YOKE—a symbol of burden, slavery, oppression; also associated with the idea of being unequally yoked in relationships and partnerships. (See Genesis 27:40; Matthew 11:29–30; 2 Corinthians 6:14.)

Z

ZACHARY—"remembered by God." The name Zachary can be seen as a spiritual reference to the importance of being remembered and loved by God.

ZANE—"God is gracious." The name Zane can be seen as a spiritual reference to the idea of grace.

ZEBRA—compared to "wild donkey" in Scripture, a zebra is often used as a symbol of freedom and wildness. (See Job 39:5–8.)

APPENDIX B: NUMBERS IN DREAMS

The following is a collection of numbers paired with their commonly held meanings based on biblical references. Numbers in your dreams may have deeper meanings, such as those mentioned above, or they may simply represent numerical values depending on the context. Though God seemed to assign consistent meaning and value to certain numbers in Scripture, it's important to ask the Holy Spirit for revelation around every part of your dream.

1. UNITY, SINGULARITY, GOD:

- Represents the oneness and unity of God. (See Deuteronomy 6:4.)
- Symbolizes the beginning and source of all creation
- In the Bible, the first commandment emphasizes the importance of worshiping only one God. (See Exodus 20:3.)
- The book of Genesis describes God creating the world out of nothing, highlighting the singularity and power of God's creative act. (See Genesis 1:1–31.)
- The number 1 is also associated with other concepts such as uniqueness, leadership, and primacy. For example, Jesus is often referred to as the "firstborn" or "*firstfruits*" of the resurrection (see 1 Corinthians 15:23), highlighting His primacy and uniqueness as the Son of God.

2. WITNESS, TESTIMONY, TWO SIDES OF A MATTER:

- Signifies the importance of witness and testimony in legal and spiritual matters, from the Ten Commandments, which required 2 witnesses for a legal matter (see Deuteronomy 19:15), to the apostles who bore witness to the resurrection of Jesus. (See Acts 1:8, 2:32.)

- Represents the idea of duality, such as light and darkness, good and evil, or heaven and earth; pairs or opposites, such as the 2 pillars in the temple (see 1 Kings 7:15–22), the 2 olive trees in Zechariah's vision (see Zechariah 4:11–14), or the 2 witnesses in Revelation. (See Revelation 11:3–12.)
- Can signify balance or harmony, such as the importance of balancing faith and works (see James 2:14–26), or the complementary nature of male and female. (See Genesis 1:27.)

3. TRINITY, DIVINE PERFECTION:

- Represents the 3 persons of the Trinity (Father, Son, and Holy Spirit).
- The number 3 is also associated with the divine attributes of perfection and completeness, such as the 3 gifts of the magi (gold, frankincense, and myrrh) given to the baby Jesus (see Matthew 2:11), or the 3 theological virtues of faith, hope, and love. (See 1 Corinthians 13:13.)
- In some cases, the number 3 may also represent the 3 dimensions of reality, such as the heavens, the earth, and the waters under the earth. (See Exodus 20:4.)

4. CREATION, THE EARTH, THE 4 CORNERS OF THE EARTH:

- Represents the 4 elements of the natural world (earth, air, fire, and water).
- Symbolizes the physical creation and the earth, as in the 4 rivers in the garden of Eden. (See Genesis 2:10–14.)
- May represent the 4 corners of the earth, as in the 4 angels standing at the 4 corners of the earth, holding back the 4 winds in Revelation. (See Revelation 7:1.)
- The number 4 is also associated with the 4 Gospels in the New Testament, which together tell the story of Jesus's life and teachings.
- In some cases, the number 4 may represent stability or structure, such as the 4 legs of the throne of God (see Ezekiel 1:5), the 4 living creatures around the throne in Revelation (see Revelation 4:6–9), or the 4 horns of the altar. (See Exodus 27:2.)

5. GRACE, GOD'S GOODNESS, HUMAN WEAKNESS:

- The number 5 often represents God's grace and provision, as in the 5 loaves used to feed the five thousand (see Matthew 14:17–21), or the 5 smooth stones that David used to defeat Goliath. (See 1 Samuel 17:40.)
- The wounds on Jesus's hands, feet, and side (5 wounds) represent His sacrificial love and the grace He extended to humanity.
- The 5 books of Moses, which make up the Pentateuch or Torah, the first 5 books of the Old Testament.
- Depending on the context, it may represent human weakness, as in the 5 foolish virgins who did not have enough oil for their lamps. (See Matthew 25:1–13.)

6. MAN, HUMAN WEAKNESS, IMPERFECTION:

- Represents humanity, as man was created on the sixth day in the biblical creation story. (See Genesis 1:26–31.)
- Symbolizes human weakness and imperfection, as in the number of man in the book of Revelation, 666. (See Revelation 13:18.)
- May represent incompleteness or a falling short of divine perfection.
- In some cases, the number 6 may also represent work or labor, as the Israelites were commanded to work for 6 days and rest on the seventh day in the Ten Commandments. (See Exodus 20:8–11.)
- Other symbolic uses of the number 6 in the Bible: Joshua and the Israelites marched around Jericho 6 days before the walls fell (see Joshua 6:3–4); Jesus turned water from 6 stone water jars at the wedding in Cana into wine. (See John 2:1–11.)

7. COMPLETION, PERFECTION, REST:

- Represents the completion or perfection of a cycle, such as the 7 days of creation or the 7 seals, trumpets, and bowls in the book of Revelation.
- May represent rest or cessation, such as the Sabbath day of rest.
- The number 7 is one of the most significant numbers in the Bible, appearing more than seven hundred times in various contexts: there are 7 colors of the rainbow (see Genesis 9:13–16), the 7 branches of

the menorah (see Exodus 25:31–40), and the 7 churches in Revelation. (See Revelation 2–3.)

- There are 7 festivals on the Jewish sacred calendar.

8. NEW BEGINNINGS, REGENERATION, RESURRECTION, EVERGREEN:

- Represents new beginnings or regeneration, as in the 8 people saved in the ark during the flood. (See Genesis 7:13; 1 Peter 3:20.)
- Circumcision on the eighth day marked the start of a covenant relationship with God. (See Genesis 17:12.)
- Symbolizes resurrection or renewal, as in the eighth day after birth when a male child was circumcised (see Genesis 17:12) and Jesus's resurrection on the first day of the week, which is referred to as the eighth day, since it breaks the seven-day cycle. (See John 20:1.)
- May represent abundance or plenty, as in the 8 days of the Feast of Tabernacles. (See Leviticus 23:33–36.)
- Also associated with new life and regeneration, evergreen trees produce fruit year-round. (See Ezekiel 47:12.)

9. FRUITFULNESS, FULLNESS, FINALITY:

- Symbolizes fruitfulness as in the fruit of the Spirit (love, joy, peace, patience, kindness, goodness, faithfulness, gentleness, and self-control). (See Galatians 5:22–23.)
- May represent increase or multiplication, as in the 9 gifts of the Spirit. (See 1 Corinthians 12:8–10.)
- Fullness of time, as in the 9 months of pregnancy.

10. DIVINE ORDER, COMPLETENESS:

- Represents divine order, as in the Ten Commandments given to Moses (see Exodus 20:1–17), the 10 plagues in Egypt bringing Israel's captivity to a close, and the 10 virgins in the parable of the wise and foolish virgins. (See Matthew 25:1–13.)

11. INCREASE, FAITH, GRACE, DISORDER, INCOMPLETENESS:

- Can represent increase or abundance, as in Joseph, who was eleventh in the birth order, who brought increase to the home of Potiphar, and also in Egypt, ultimately becoming a ruler in Egypt. (See Genesis 37–50.)
- In Hebrews 11, the "hall of faith," the number 11 represents the faith of those who trusted in God.
- In Jesus's parable of the vineyard workers found in Matthew 20, some translations use the phrase *"eleventh hour"* to describe the time of day when the landowner hires more workers for his vineyard, who are later paid the same as those who worked a full day, emphasizing Jesus's message of grace versus the law.
- Symbolizes incompleteness or the need for further development, as in the 11 apostles who remained after the betrayal of Judas. (See Acts 1:15–26.)
- May represent the tension between the divine and the earthly, as 11 is one more than 10, the number of divine order.

12. GOVERNMENTAL AUTHORITY, DIVINE ORDER:

- Symbolizes governmental order and authority, as in the 12 tribes of Israel, the 12 apostles chosen by Jesus, the 12 gates, and the 12 foundations of the new Jerusalem. (See Revelation 21:12–14.)
- In addition to the examples above, other uses of the number 12 in the Bible include the 12 stones that Joshua set up as a memorial after crossing the Jordan River (see Joshua 4:1–9) and the 12 spies sent to scout the promised land. (See Numbers 13:1–33.)

13. REBELLION, REDEMPTION, DESTRUCTION, CONSTRUCTION, JOY, DISORDER:

- Based on the Bible's first mention of the number 13, it's usually associated with rebellion. *"Twelve years they served Chedorlaomer, and in the thirteenth year they rebelled"* (Genesis 14:4 NKJV).

However, though it's not mentioned often in Scripture, there are other mentions that may have different associations for the number:

- Thirteen years after Hagar gave birth to Ishmael (representing Abraham's self-effort to bring about God's promise), God spoke to Abraham, promising that his covenant would come through the family line he would establish through Sarah and her son (representing grace).
- The people of Israel marched around the walls of Jericho 13 times in total—once a day for six days, and seven times on the seventh day—before shouting and seeing the walls fall.
- According to 1 Kings 7:1, Solomon took 13 years to build his palace, which can be seen as a significant period of construction and completion.
- In Judaism, the number 13 represents celebration and joy, as a 13-year-old boy becomes a bar mitzvah.
- The number 13 may represent the tension between divine and human systems, as 13 is one more than twelve, the number of divine government.

14. DELIVERANCE, SALVATION, DOUBLE MEASURE:

- In Matthew 1:1–17, Matthew divides the genealogy of Jesus into three sets of 14 generations: 14 generations from Abraham to David, 14 generations from David to the Babylonian exile, and 14 generations from the Babylonian exile to Christ.
- Fourteen is double the number 7 (wholeness, rest).
- God instructs Israel to celebrate Passover on the fourteenth day of the first month. (See Numbers 28:16–25.)

15. REST, INCREASE:

- God instructs the Feast of Tabernacles to begin on the fifteenth day of the seventh month, starting with a day of rest. (See Leviticus 23:34–36.)
- In 2 Kings 20:4–6, God hears King Hezekiah's prayers and adds 15 years to his life, and promises to deliver him from the Assyrians.

17. SPIRITUAL PERFECTION, CLEANSING, LAW:

- Ten (divine order) plus seven (completion) equals 17.

- The number 17 is used more than once in the story of Noah: the rain began on the seventeenth day of the month (see Genesis 7:11); on the seventeenth day of the seventh month, the ark came to rest on the mountains of Ararat. (See Genesis 8:4.)
- May represent the idea of law or commandment, as 17 is the sum of ten and seven, which represent the Ten Commandments and the sevenfold Spirit of God, respectively.

18. LIFE, BLESSING, JUDGMENT:

- Symbolizes blessing or prosperity, as in the Hebrew word for "life" (*chai*), which has a numerical value of 18 and is sometimes used as a symbol of good luck or blessing.
- May be seen as symbolizing this idea of future glory in the midst of present suffering. Just as the apostle Paul writes in Romans 8:18 that the sufferings of this present time are not worth comparing to the glory that will be revealed, so too the number 18 may be seen as representing the hope and assurance that believers have amid their struggles.
- May represent judgment or bondage, as in the eighteenth chapter of the book of Revelation, which describes the fall of Babylon the Great and the judgment of the wicked.

20. WAITING, EXPECTANCY, COMPLETION:

- Jacob toiled for Laban for 20 years while waiting for what was promised to him. (See Genesis 31:38–42.)
- Symbolizes expectancy, as in the twentieth year of King Artaxerxes, when Nehemiah was allowed to return to Jerusalem to rebuild the walls. (See Nehemiah 2:1–8.)
- May represent completion, as 20 is the product of two multiplied by ten (completeness).

21. FULLNESS, WAITING, COMPLETION:

- May represent the idea of fullness or completion, as 21 is the product of three multiplied by seven. (See Exodus 12:18.)
- Daniel waited 21 days for an answer from God. (See Daniel 10:13.)

22. INCREASE, REVELATION, APOSTOLIC AUTHORITY:

- Twenty-two is the product of eleven multiplied by two, so we can look at this number as a "doubling" of the number 11, which can represent an increase.
- Symbolizes revelation or insight, the book of Revelation has 22 chapters; some scholars believe that the number 22 represents completeness or fullness of prophetic revelation.
- May represent apostolic authority or leadership, as in the 22 letters of the Hebrew alphabet, which are sometimes associated with the idea of divine communication and authority.

24. PRIESTHOOD, GOVERNMENTAL PERFECTION/ORDER, WHOLENESS:

- Represents the priesthood, as in the 24 divisions of the priests established by King David (see 1 Chronicles 24:1–19) and the 24 elders who worship around the throne of God night and day in the book of Revelation. (See Revelation 4:4–11.)
- Governmental perfection, as in a doubling of the number 12.
- In some Jewish and Christian traditions, the number 24 is associated with the idea of "completeness" or "wholeness," as it represents the number of books in the Jewish canon.

25. GRACE, FORGIVENESS, ATONEMENT:

- The fullness of the grace of God, as in the product of 25 (five multiplied by five)—grace upon grace.

26. YHWH, GOD:

- According to Hebrew numerology, the numerical value of the name of God in Hebrew, represented by the letters Yod, He, Waw, He (YHWH), is 26; calculated by adding the numerical values of each letter: 10 (Yod) plus 5 (He) plus 6 (Waw) plus 5 (He) equals 26.
- Also, when assigning each letter a numerical value based on its alphabetical position (A equals 1, B equals 2, and so on), the English word "GOD" sums up to 26: G equals 7, O equals 15, and D equals 4, which adds to 26.

30. MATURITY, RIGHT TIMING TO LEAD/REIGN, MINISTRY:

- Joseph was 30 years old when he left prison and entered the service of Pharaoh. (See Genesis 41:46.)
- Entering into full-time ministry or service to God, as Jesus began His public ministry at 30 years of age, when He was baptized by John the Baptist (see Luke 3:23); priests could begin their service at the age of 30. (See Numbers 4:3.)
- Symbolizes dedication or consecration, as in the thirtieth chapter of the book of Exodus, which describes the laws of vows and dedications and the consequences of breaking them. (See Exodus 30:11–16.)

40. TESTING, PREPARATION, CLEANSING, RULING:

- Represents the idea of testing or trial, as in the 40 days and nights that Jesus spent fasting and praying in the wilderness before beginning His public ministry. (See Matthew 4:1–11.)
- Symbolizes the idea of preparation, as in the 40 years that the Israelites spent wandering in the wilderness after leaving Egypt. During that time, they were prepared and purified for the promised land. (See Numbers 14:33–34.)
- May represent the idea of judgment or cleansing, as in the 40 days of rain that caused the flood in the time of Noah, which cleansed the wickedness of humanity. (See Genesis 7:4.)
- Moses spent 40 days on Mount Sinai receiving the Law from God. (See Exodus 24:18; Exodus 34:28.)
- Both King David (see 2 Samuel 5:4) and King Solomon ruled for 40 years, during which Israel was established as a major power. (See 1 Kings 11:42–43.)

41. NEW BEGINNING, VICTORY:

- In some Jewish and Christian traditions, the number 41 is associated with the idea of "victory" or "conquest," as it represents the Israelites entering the promised land after wandering for 40 years. It may symbolize the concept of overcoming obstacles and claiming the promises of God. As the "first day" out of the wilderness, which is a time of preparation, testing, and growth, 41 represents a new beginning, a time of exiting the wilderness and entering into a new season. In this sense, the number 41 can represent a time of transition, of leaving behind the old and moving into the new.

50. RESTORATION, FORGIVENESS, JUBILEE:

- God instructs Israel to set aside the year after the forty-ninth year as a "Jubilee" as a time to reset the land, forgive debts, and release enslaved people. (See Leviticus 25:8–13.)

70. PERFECT SPIRITUAL ORDER, LIFETIME/GENERATION:

- Seventy is the product of seven multiplied by ten.
- Total number of members in Joseph's family. (See Genesis 46:27.)
- There were 70 elders appointed to assist Moses in the governance of the people. (See Numbers 11:16–17.)
- An average lifespan, as in Psalm 90:10: *"Our days may come to seventy years"* (NIV).

77. TOTAL FORGIVENESS, PERFECTION, DIVINE INHERITANCE:

- Represents the idea of completeness or wholeness, as in the 77 times that Jesus tells Peter to forgive his brother (see Matthew 18:21–22), indicating the importance of complete forgiveness and reconciliation.
- May represent the idea of divine inheritance, as 77 is the product of seven (the number of divine perfection) and eleven (the number of increase); may symbolize the idea of receiving the fullness of God's inheritance and revelation.

100. FULLNESS OR COMPLETENESS:

- Abraham's age: In Genesis 17:17, God promises Abraham that he and his wife Sarah will have a son, even though they are both advanced in age. When Isaac is born, Abraham is 100 years old (see Genesis 21:5), which is seen as a sign of God's faithfulness and the fulfillment of His promises.
- The 100-fold blessing: In the parable of the sower (see Mark 4:3–9; Matthew 13:3–9; Luke 8:5–8), Jesus tells of a farmer who sows his seed and some falls on good soil, producing a crop that yields thirty, sixty, or even 100 times what was sown. This is seen as a symbol of

the abundance and fruitfulness that God can bring to the lives of those who receive His Word.

- The 100 sheep: In the parable of the lost sheep (see Luke 15:4–7; Matthew 18:12–14), Jesus tells of a shepherd who leaves his ninety-nine sheep to search for one that is lost. When he finds the lost sheep, he rejoices and calls on his friends and neighbors to join him in celebration. This parable is a picture of God's love and concern for each person, as well as His willingness to go to great lengths to rescue those who are lost.

400. DELIVERANCE, FREEDOM, AND THE FULFILLMENT OF GOD'S PROMISES:

- The number of years that the Israelites were in bondage in Egypt, until their deliverance, according to the prophecy given to Abraham. (See Genesis 15:13–16.)
- The number of years of the Intertestamental Period, during which time there were no inspired prophetic voices recorded in the Bible, until John the Baptist began prophesying about the coming Messiah. (See John 1:6–8.)

APPENDIX C: FURTHER READINGS AND SCRIPTURE PASSAGES

READINGS

The Divinity Code to Understanding Your Dreams and Visions by Adam Thompson and Adrian Beale. This is my favorite dream resource and one of the few books I keep on my nightstand. It not only offers comprehensive Bible-based teaching on the act of interpreting dreams and visions but also features an extensive dictionary with thousands of themes, objects, names, places, and numbers, along with their scriptural definitions and origins.

The Dream Book: A Simple Guide for Interpreting Your Dreams by Steven Maddox. Mentored by John Paul Jackson, Steven Maddox has spent decades studying and interpreting dreams, pioneering dream interpretation as a form of evangelism in the mid-1990s. He has interpreted tens of thousands of dreams and facilitates workshops on dream interpretation. In *The Dream Book,* he addresses fundamental questions about the origins, purposes, and types of dreams, aiming to simplify dream interpretation and make it accessible.

Dream Language: The Prophetic Power of Dreams, Revelations, and the Spirit of Wisdom by James Goll and Michal Ann Goll. This is one of the first books I ever read that taught about the "language" of dreams, and I consider it a must-read for any avid dreamer.

Numbers That Preach: Understanding God's Mathematical Lingo by Troy A. Brewer. Pastor Troy Brewer takes a deep dive into the biblical significance of various numbers that may appear in our dreams or in everyday life, revealing the meanings behind Scripture's many numerical references. He also has video teachings available on his website, PropheticNumbers.com.

The Ultimate Guide to Understanding the Dreams You Dream: Biblical Keys for Hearing God's Voice in the Night by Ira Milligan. Drawing on decades of experience, Milligan provides scriptural insights, personal examples, and a detailed dictionary of dream symbols to help readers discern divine messages received during sleep.

SCRIPTURES

And he dreamed, and behold, a ladder set up on the earth, and the top of it reached to heaven; and behold, the angels of God were ascending and descending on it. —Genesis 28:12 KJ21

Joseph had a dream, and when he told it to his brothers, they hated him all the more. He said to them, "Listen to this dream I had: We were binding sheaves of grain out in the field when suddenly my sheaf rose and stood upright, while your sheaves gathered around mine and bowed down to it." —Genesis 37:5–7 NIV

When two full years had passed, Pharaoh had a dream: He was standing by the Nile, when out of the river there came up seven cows, sleek and fat, and they grazed among the reeds. After them, seven other cows, ugly and gaunt, came up out of the Nile and stood beside those on the riverbank. And the cows that were ugly and gaunt ate up the seven sleek, fat cows. Then Pharaoh woke up. He fell asleep again and had a second dream: Seven heads of grain, healthy and good, were growing on a single stalk. After them, seven other heads of grain sprouted—thin and scorched by the east wind. The thin heads of grain swallowed up the seven healthy, full heads. Then Pharaoh woke up; it had been a dream. In the morning his mind was troubled, so he sent for all the magicians and wise men of Egypt. Pharaoh told them his dreams, but no one could interpret them for him. —Genesis 41:1–8 NIV

Pharaoh said to Joseph, "I had a dream, and no one can interpret it. But I have heard it said of you that when you hear a dream you can interpret it." "I cannot do it," Joseph replied to Pharaoh, "but God will give Pharaoh the answer he desires." —Genesis 41:15–16 NIV

I will give you hidden treasures, riches stored in secret places, so that you may know that I am the LORD, the God of Israel, who summons you by name. —Isaiah 45:3 NIV

Seek the LORD while he may be found; call on him while he is near. —Isaiah 55:6 NIV

Ask me and I will tell you remarkable secrets you do not know about things to come. —Jeremiah 33:3 NLT

Then Daniel praised the God of heaven and said: "Praise be to the name of God for ever and ever; wisdom and power are his. He changes times and seasons; he deposes kings and raises up others. He gives wisdom to the wise and knowledge to the discerning. He reveals deep and hidden things; he knows what lies in darkness, and light dwells with him. I thank and praise you, God of my ancestors: You have given me wisdom and power, you have made known to me what we asked of you, you have made known to us the dream of the king." —Daniel 2:19–23 NIV

Daniel replied, "No wise man, enchanter, magician or diviner can explain to the king the mystery he has asked about, but there is a God in heaven who reveals mysteries. He has shown King Nebuchadnezzar what will happen in days to come. Your dream and the visions that passed through your mind as you were lying in bed are these." —Daniel 2:27–28 NIV

I will pour out my Spirit on all people. Your sons and daughters will prophesy, your old men will dream dreams, and your young men will see visions. —Joel 2:28 NIV

But after he had considered this, an angel of the Lord appeared to him in a dream and said, "Joseph son of David, do not be afraid to take Mary home as your wife, because what is conceived in her is from the Holy Spirit. She will give birth to a son, and you are to give him the name Jesus, because he will save his people from their sins." All this took place to fulfill what the Lord had said through the prophet. —Matthew 1:20–22 NIV

Keep asking, and it will be given to you. Keep searching, and you will find. Keep knocking, and the door will be opened to you. For everyone who asks, receives, and the one who searches finds, and to the one who knocks, the door will be opened. —Matthew 7:7–8 HCSB

If from there you seek the LORD your God, you will find him if you seek him with all your heart and with all your soul.

—Deuteronomy 4:29 NIV

He who dwells in the secret place of the Most High shall abide under the shadow of the Almighty. —Psalm 91:1 NKJV

I will give you hidden treasures, riches stored in secret places, so that you may know that I am the LORD, the God of Israel, who summons you by name. —Isaiah 45:3 NIV

The secret things belong to the LORD our God, but the things that are revealed belong to us and to our children forever.

—Deuteronomy 29:29 ESV

God conceals the revelation of his word in the hiding place of his glory. But the honor of kings is revealed by how they thoroughly search out the deeper meaning of all that God says. —Proverbs 25:2

In a dream, a vision of the night [one may hear God's voice], when deep sleep falls on men, while slumbering upon the bed, then He opens the ears of men and seals their instruction. —Job 33:15–16 AMP

While he was still debating with himself about what to do, he fell asleep and had a supernatural dream. An angel from the Lord appeared to him and said, "Joseph, descendant of David, don't hesitate to take Mary into your home as your wife, because the power of the Holy Spirit has conceived a child in her womb. She will give birth to a son and you are to name him 'Savior,' for he is destined to give his life to save his people from their sins."

This happened to fulfill what the Lord had spoken through his prophet: Listen! A virgin will be pregnant, she will give birth to a Son, and he will be known as "Emmanuel," which means in Hebrew, "God became one of us." When Joseph woke from his dream, he did all that the angel of the Lord instructed him to do. He took Mary to be his wife.

—Matthew 1:20–24

And having been warned in a dream not to go back to Herod, they returned to their country by another route. When they had gone, an angel of the Lord appeared to Joseph in a dream. "Get up," he said, "take the child and his mother and escape to Egypt. Stay there until I tell you, for Herod is going to search for the child to kill him."

—Matthew 2:12–13 NIV

Just then, as Pilate was presiding over the tribunal, his wife sent him an urgent message: "Don't harm that holy man, for I suffered a horrible nightmare last night about him!" —Matthew 27:19

About noon the following day as they were on their journey and approaching the city, Peter went up on the roof to pray. He became hungry and wanted something to eat, and while the meal was being prepared, he fell into a trance. He saw heaven opened and something like a large sheet being let down to earth by its four corners. It contained all kinds of four-footed animals, as well as reptiles and birds. Then a voice told him, "Get up, Peter. Kill and eat." "Surely not, Lord!" Peter replied. "I have never eaten anything impure or unclean." The voice spoke to him a second time, "Do not call anything impure that God has made clean."

—Acts 10:9–15 NIV

During the night Paul had a vision of a man of Macedonia standing and begging him, "Come over to Macedonia and help us." After Paul had seen the vision, we got ready at once to leave for Macedonia, concluding that God had called us to preach the gospel to them. —Acts 16:9–10 NIV

For God's angel visited me last night, the angel of my God, the God I passionately serve. He came and stood in front of me and said, "Don't be afraid, Paul. You are destined to stand trial before Caesar. And because of God's favor on you, he has given you the lives of everyone who is sailing with you." So men, keep up your courage! I know that God will protect you, just as he told me he would. —Acts 27:23–25

I must go on boasting. Although there is nothing to be gained, I will go on to visions and revelations from the Lord. I know a man in Christ who fourteen years ago was caught up to the third heaven. Whether it was in the body or out of the body I do not know—God knows. And I know that this man—whether in the body or apart from the body I do not know, but God knows—was caught up to paradise and heard inexpressible things, things that no one is permitted to tell. —2 Corinthians 12:1–4 NIV

On the Lord's Day I was in the Spirit, and I heard behind me a loud voice like a trumpet, which said: "Write on a scroll what you see and send it to the seven churches: to Ephesus, Smyrna, Pergamum, Thyatira, Sardis, Philadelphia and Laodicea." I turned around to see the voice that was speaking to me. And when I turned I saw seven golden lampstands, and among the lampstands was someone like a son of man, dressed in a robe reaching down to his feet and with a golden sash around his chest. The hair on his head was white like wool, as white as snow, and his eyes were like blazing fire. His feet were like bronze glowing in a furnace, and his voice was like the sound of rushing waters. In his right hand he held seven stars, and coming out of his mouth was a sharp, double-edged sword. His face was like the sun shining in all its brilliance. When I saw him, I fell at his feet as though dead. Then he placed his right hand on me and said: "Do not be afraid. I am the First and the Last. I am the Living One; I was dead, and now look, I am alive for ever and ever! And I hold the keys of death and Hades." —Revelation 1:9–18

APPENDIX D: WORLD-CHANGING CHRISTIANS WHO WERE IMPACTED BY DREAMS

As we've identified, dreaming was not just for those living in Bible times. If you need proof, here's a brief roundup of world-changing Christian leaders, pastors, and pioneers of the faith, from post-biblical into modern history, whose lives and ministries were impacted by their dreams.

ST. AUGUSTINE:

The famous theologian and bishop had an experience one evening during a time of great distress and prayer, during which he heard a child's voice say, "Pick it up, read it. Pick it up, read it," which he took as a sign to read the Bible and begin his journey to faith.

ST. FRANCIS OF ASSISI:

The Italian friar and founder of the Franciscan Order was renowned for his dedication to poverty, his love for creation, and his profound spiritual devotion. Early in his life, he had a dream of a grand palace filled with armor, which he initially *misinterpreted* as a call to become a knight, destined for worldly glory—a calling he initially pursued. But while he was on his way to join a military campaign in southern Italy, God issued a course-correction when Francis had a dream in which God asked, "Who do you serve, the servant or the master?" It was then that Francis began to question his ambitions. Through a period of reflection and prayer, he came to understand his true calling—to serve Christ and dedicate himself to a life of humility and spiritual renewal. Later in life, he had a vision at the church of San Damiano, where

Christ spoke to him from a crucifix, saying, "Rebuild My church." Francis repaired the physical building but then understood the vision as more of a call to renew the church spiritually. These, and other experiences, inspired Francis's life of humility and service.

JOHN NEWTON:

In a letter to a friend, the former slave trader and author of the hymn "Amazing Grace" recounts a vivid dream in which he is entrusted with a ring, symbolizing God's mercy and favor, with the condition that his happiness depends on keeping it safe. Under the influence of a tempter, he doubts the ring's power and drops it into the sea, triggering a vision of fiery mountains, symbolizing judgment and despair. Overwhelmed by regret, Newton is then rescued by a third figure, likely Christ, who retrieves the ring and extinguishes the flames but refuses to return it, promising to safeguard it on his behalf. The dream illustrated for Newton the assurance of God's divine grace. He wrote to his friend, "O what an unspeakable comfort is this, that I am not in mine own keeping! The Lord is my shepherd."

SOJOURNER TRUTH:

Born Isabella in 1797, the nineteenth-century African-American abolitionist and women's rights activist reported that Jesus appeared to her in a life-changing vision during her journey to freedom. In 1827, shortly after escaping slavery, she was saved from returning to her former master's farm by a vivid and terrifying vision of God, followed by the calming presence of Jesus, whom she recognized as her protector, and she then reported being "baptized by the Holy Spirit." This encounter gave her the courage to overcome fear and trust fully in God's guidance. The vision became a cornerstone of her faith, empowering her to fight for justice, preach boldly, and embrace her calling as an advocate for truth, freedom, and faith in Jesus Christ.

AIMEE SEMPLE MCPHERSON:

The Pentecostal evangelist and founder of the Foursquare Church reportedly had a vision in 1918 while praying over her daughter, in which God told her He would give her a home in California. In October 1918, McPherson and her family drove from New York to Los Angeles over a period of two months, during which McPherson preached revivals along the way. McPherson's first revival in Los Angeles was held at Victoria Hall, a one-thousand-seat auditorium downtown. In 1923, she opened the 5,300-seat Angelus Temple, now known as The Dream Center.

CORRIE TEN BOOM:

In her remarkable book *The Hiding Place*, the Dutch Christian author and Holocaust survivor shares a terrifying prophetic dream she had as a child in which she saw a black horse-drawn wagon carrying her, her father, her sister Betsie, and other family members, friends, and strangers across the city square. They were unable to escape. Upon sharing the dream with Betsie, her sister replied, "If God has shown us bad times ahead, it's enough for me that He knows about them. That's why He sometimes shows us things, you know—to tell us that this too is in His hands."[1] Indeed, the dream came to pass when the Ten Boom family, known for hiding Jews in their home during the Nazi occupation of the Netherlands, was arrested by the Gestapo.

C. S. LEWIS:

The beloved author of *The Chronicles of Narnia* wrote that he was dreaming frequently of lions at the time he was writing the stories, which inspired the creation of the character Aslan. It was only later that he connected the symbolism between Aslan and Christ. "At first I had very little idea how the story would go. But then suddenly Aslan came bounding into it. I think I had been having a good many dreams of lions about that time. Apart from that, I don't know where the lion came from or why He came. But once He was there he pulled the whole story together, and soon He pulled the six other Narnian stories in after Him."[2]

REINHARD BONNKE:

Reinhard Bonnke founded Christ for All Nations in 1972 following several powerful and recurring dreams. While visiting Africa, Reinhard had a dream in which the African continent was washed in the blood of Jesus, and he heard the Lord say, "All Africa shall be saved!" This dream happened night after night, inspiring him to found Christ for All Nations and fueling his passion for evangelism on the continent. More than seventy-nine million salvations were recorded during his lifetime. In a second dream near the end of his ministry, Reinhard saw himself as a forerunner of a generation of

---

1. Corrie ten Boom, Elizabeth Sherrill, and John L. Sherrill, *The Hiding Place*, 35th anniversary ed. (Chosen Books, 2006), 54.
2. C. S. Lewis, *Of This and Other Worlds*, ed. Walter Hooper (Collins, 1982), 64.

Holy Spirit-empowered evangelists, leading him to focus on equipping others to carry on the mission. Then, shortly before Reinhard's passing, Daniel Kolenda, president of Christ for All Nations and a fellow evangelist, had a dream of a "decade of double harvest," envisioning God doubling the number of souls saved and igniting an unprecedented global evangelistic movement. Dreams propelled Christ for All Nations into existence and have fueled a new era of global impact.

NABEEL QURESHI:

Formerly a devout Muslim, Nabeel Qureshi shared that God gave him dreams that led him to embrace Christianity. In a personal account for *Christianity Today,* he wrote, "By the end of my first year in medical school, God had given me a vision and three dreams, the second of which was the most powerful. In it I was standing at the threshold of a strikingly narrow door, watching people take their seats at a wedding feast. I desperately wanted to get in, but I was not able to enter, because I had yet to accept my friend David's invitation to the wedding. When I awoke, I knew what God was telling me, but I sought further verification. It was then that I found the parable of the narrow door, in Luke 13:22–30. God was showing me where I stood."[3] His story can be read in his book *Seeking Allah, Finding Jesus.*

TOM DOYLE:

A longtime missionary to the Middle East, Tom Doyle has spent years documenting accounts of Jesus appearing to Muslims in dreams and visions, calling them to believe in Him in a culture where Christianity is forbidden. He shares a collection of stories in his book *Dreams and Visions: Is Jesus Awakening the Muslim World?*

BETH MOORE:

Bestselling author and Bible teacher Beth Moore shared a meaningful dream she had after the tragic loss of Maria Chapman, the young daughter of Mary Beth and Steven Curtis Chapman. In the dream, Beth saw herself in an arena, not as the speaker, but watching Mary Beth, accompanied by Maria, taking the stage to minister. She awakened from the dream with a sense that it meant something. "I thought maybe it was God showing me that part of [the

---

3. Nabeel Qureshi, "Christ Called Me Off the Minaret," *Christianity Today,* January 29, 2014, accessed July 16, 2025, https://www.christianitytoday.com/2014/01/christ-called-me-off-minaret/.

Chapmans'] healing and specifically, Mary Beth Chapman's healing, would be that she would minister hope through what she had been through," she shared with an audience on *Life Today*. "I knew that the symbol of [Maria] in the dream was redemption and healing—that there would be healing to [Mary Beth's] soul and that their joyous memories would be restored."[4] When Beth shared the dream with Mary Beth, she discovered that on the same night, Mary Beth had prayed for a dream about Maria. The dream confirmed to Mary Beth that God was calling her to speak and share her journey of healing.

CHRISTINE CAINE:

The Australian preacher, bestselling author, and founder of anti-trafficking initiative A21 has shared about having a dream in which she vividly saw a group of girls in a sealed container, screaming for help. She recounts that when she woke up, she was soaked with sweat, and her own voice was screaming back, "I hear you! We're coming to get you! We're coming to get you!" She said, "Any time when I think the work we're doing with A21 is just too hard, I remember that dream. God spoke to me, I heard their cries." She describes another experience earlier in life, before she began her preaching ministry, in which she had an open vision while fully awake. She was attending a sporting event in a large arena but recalls that everything seemed to stop around her: "I was moved from my seat to a platform, and that whole arena was listening and I was proclaiming the gospel. And I just saw streams of people coming forward to say yes to Jesus." To this day, when preaching to large crowds, before Caine steps onto the platform she prays, "Holy Spirit, You showed me this."[5]

---

4. Beth Moore, "The Dream," *Life Today*, May 17, 2012, https://www.youtube.com/watch?v=OOgSNnkTFfI.
5. Christine Caine, "The Holy Spirit in Your Dreams," *Better Together on TBN*, September 5, 2020, https://www.youtube.com/watch?v=uh468zu40A4.

ABOUT THE AUTHOR

PAIGE COLLINS is a lifelong dreamer and visionary entrepreneur, and is the founding partner of Icon Media Group, a premier PR firm specializing in faith and family entertainment. With over twenty-five years of strategic communications expertise, Paige has spearheaded high-impact publicity campaigns for major faith-based film releases, as well as for kingdom-driven nonprofits and brands, producing red-carpet premieres, intimate press conferences, and behind-the-scenes media experiences. Beyond publicity, Paige is a multifaceted creative professional, serving as both a film producer and screenwriter, leading her own film and television development company—a calling she received in a dream.